chilli to vanilla

FAUCHON
the recipes

chilli to vanilla

text
MARIE ABADIE
photography
JEAN-PIERRE DIETERLEN
stylist
MARIANNE PAQUIN
translation
LAURA WASHBURN

HACHETTE
Illustrated

) contents

COMESTIBLES · CAVES · DESSERTS

FAUCHON

) introduction

THE SPICE TRADE HAD BEEN FIRMLY ESTABLISHED by the end of the nineteenth century. It began in the Middle Ages, when greengrocers started selling "species aromatica", thus encroaching upon the apothecary's trade. There was a great deal of rivalry between the merchant who sold peppers, cloves, cinnamon and nutmeg, and other flavour enhancing ingredients for food, including sugar, and the one who used them in blends as medication, to heal and aid digestion.

Spice merchants had representatives at colonial trading posts; some even boarded the trading ships themselves. The spice trade was highly profitable and some tried to make it more so by adding to the weight of spice bundles with stones and debris. By the eighteenth century the two professions were clearly defined, but the demand for spices had also begun to dwindle.

The advent of a rail network across Europe in the nineteenth century facilitated trade between countries. Perishable goods were no longer as fragile thanks to the sterilisation method invented by Nicolas Appert. Exotic ingredients arrived from faraway lands and International Expositions broadened horizons.

From a Paris teeming with merchants and showmen emerged a middle class clientele, who owed their fortunes to the industrial revolution and the beginnings of colonialism. They were hungry for novelty and this sparked new interest in all things exotic, including spices.

Greengrocers were all too ready to comply with demand. In London, Amsterdam and Paris, it was the birth of the department store, with its vast array of merchandise and anything one could wish to buy.

It was in just such a store in Paris, belonging to Felix Potin, that the young Auguste Fauchon began his apprenticeship. The shop sold all the household staples, of course, but they also stocked frivolous, luxury items; more than shopkeepers, they were dream merchants.

During this period, Auguste Fauchon was pushing his costermonger's barrow through the gas-lit streets of Paris, selling the finest fruit and vegetables that France had to offer. In 1886, when he was 30 years old, he knew what his ambition was: to become the finest greengrocer in France. He opened his first shop in the Place de la Madeleine, in Paris, just a stone's throw from the opera house and the *grands boulevards*. In 1890, he added a wine cellar. In 1895, he expanded further, adding a bakery and 1898 saw the opening of his tea room, the *Grand Salon de Thé*.

With an insatiable appetite, Fauchon sought out the finest products, whether they came from the biggest international wholesaler or the smallest French producer hidden away deep in the countryside. Already the array of spices included many different types of black peppercorn; ground in varying degrees, as well as cloves, whole nutmegs sold individually, cinnamon sticks, etc. The shop exuded the gentle aroma of vanilla, available as superior, best quality, luxury or ground, which mingled with the strong scent of freshly ground coffee, also available in many different types. Coffee and spices alike were all sold in the same container: a hermetically sealed tin. A greengrocer is also a keeper of flavours and the best way to do this is with high quality packaging.

Rows of bottles and pots lined the long wooden counters of the shop, containing rose-scented sweets, liquorice, barley sugar, at least 30 different kinds of biscuits, candied fruit, sugar imported from the colonies, jams and jellies, chocolates and teas. Alongside these were a multitude of other delights, including home-made fruit preserves, mustards, pickles and "English" curry powders.

A photo from 1900 shows about 40 shop employees. This number quickly increased when Fauchon expanded, adding a ready-prepared meals counter and a host of chefs, who quickly became part of Fauchon's unique and individual approach to his trade.

As did all greengrocers of that era, Fauchon sold lights and lighting, household cleaning necessities as well as toiletry items and a host of other daily staples: candles, petrol, Swedish matches, men's cologne, face powder for ladies, plus waters scented with balm, anise or mint for the faint-hearted.

Today, Fauchon remains faithful to its founder's traditions. It still strives to find and obtain the finest ingredients from all over the world.

The modernised spice counter offers 96 different spices from all five continents. Red, yellow or brown; ground or whole, they diffuse an enveloping aroma of pepper, anise, chilli, tropical wood, mellow pods and sweet flowers. All have been chosen for their outstanding quality.

The chefs and bakers, who continue to have an increasing role, have tested and tasted them all, looking, touching and sniffing, like fine wines. Their choices reflect the best on offer, always placing freshness and flavour highest on their list of requirements, so the end product brings an explosion of taste that lingers pleasantly.

All the spices are sold in airtight containers, waiting for a seasoned hand to release and include them in a gourmet meal.

To maintain the flavour of their essential oils, always store the spices in a cool, dry place, away from direct light.

Fauchon and his 50 chefs are pleased to share their recipes. Each spice finds pride of place, either alone, or in the company of others. Without further ado, let us, fellow armchair traveller, take you on a voyage to discover the spices of the world.

cocktails

& nibbles

Champagne Cocktail
with Orange and Pepper

Preparation: 5 minutes
(2 hours in advance)
Serves 4-6

I bottle brut champagne,
chilled
6 oranges for juicing
1/2 vanilla pod
Whole white Muntauk
peppercorns

Spice notes
**Pepper lends pazzaz and a hint
of spice to this sparkling
and refreshing combination,
ideal for any festive occasion.
Strawberry and raspberry
juices are also delicious with
champagne. If using in place
of the orange juice, replace
the Muntauk pepper with
Sarawak pepper, which blends
to woodsy and fiery perfection
with the berries.**

I
With a juicer, squeeze the juice from the oranges.
Split the vanilla pod and scrape the black seeds into
the orange juice. Refrigerate for 2 hours.

2
Fill 4-6 champagne glasses halfway with the orange
juice mix, then top up each with champagne. Give
a twist of the peppermill over each glass and serve.

CHEF'S ADVICE
*Three oranges will yield about 250 ml/9 fl oz of juice. You can
also use store-bought freshly squeezed orange juice.*

Five-Berry Crackers

**Preparation: 30 minutes
(1 hour in advance for the dough)
Cooking time: 8-10 minutes
Serves 4-6**

FOR THE CRACKERS
250 g/9 oz plain flour
1 teaspoon baking soda
Ground coriander
Five-Berry Mixture
65 g/2 oz unsalted
butter, softened
1 teaspoon salt
40 g/2 1/2 oz grated
cheese, preferably
Emmenthal

FOR THE GLAZE
1 egg yolk
Salt

Spice notes
**The flowery, woodsy blend of
Five-Berry (black pepper,
white pepper, allspice, green
peppercorns, pink peppercorns
and whole coriander seeds)
is heightened by the butteriness
of the crackers. This is the ideal
aperitif nibble to start the
gustatory juices flowing.**

1
In the bowl of an electric mixer, combine the flour, baking soda, 2 pinches ground coriander and 5-6 grinds of Five-Berry Mixture. Add the butter, grated cheese and salt and stir until the mixture resembles coarse crumbs.

2
Add 100-125 ml (3 1/2-4 fl oz) water and continue mixing until the dough just holds together and is smooth; do not overmix. Shape into a ball, cover with plastic wrap and refrigerate for 1 hour.

3
Preheat the oven to 210° C/410° F/gas 7. Line a baking tray with baking parchment. Roll the dough out about 3 mm 1/8 in thick. Use a round cutter about 2.5 cm (1 in) in diameter to stamp out dough circles. Arrange the dough circles on the tray.

4
For the glaze, beat the egg yolk with some water and a pinch of salt. With a pastry brush, coat the surface of each dough circle with some of the glaze. Give a few twists of the peppermill over each dough circle. Bake for 8-10 minutes.

CHEF'S ADVICE
To keep the crackers crispy, transfer them (still on the paper) straight from the oven to a cooling rack. These go well with Bloody Mary's, served plain or with toppings such as tapenade, sun-dried tomatoes, puréed peppers, etc.

Bloody Mary

Preparation: 5 minutes
Serves 1

60 ml/2 fl oz vodka
150 ml/5 fl oz
tomato juice
3 ice cubes
Ground chilli
Celery salt
Juice of 1/2 lemon

In a shaker, combine the vodka, tomato juice and ice cubes. Season with 2 pinches of ground chilli, 2-3 pinches celery salt and the lemon juice. Shake vigorously. Delicious served with Five-Berry Crackers (see page 14).

CHEF'S ADVICE
The intense red colour of a bloody mary comes from store-bought tomato juice. If using fresh tomato juice, stir in a bit of tomato concentrate to deepen the colour.

Spice notes
In this recipe, the more spicy, flowery taste of ground chilli replaces the traditional Tabasco sauce. Celery salt adds a hint of bitterness which is perfect for sparking the appetite.

Vodka and Sarawak Pepper Sorbet

Preparation: 10 minutes
Cooking time: 2 minutes
Makes about 600 ml/1 pint

1/2 lemon
1/4 orange
150 g/5 oz acacia honey
1 level teaspoon
agar-agar
100 ml/3 1/2 fl oz
vodka (Dubrowska)
Whole black Sarawak
peppercorns

Spice notes
**Sarawak peppercorns lend an
extraordinary woodsy and fiery,
smoldering aroma that is tinged
with the scent of dried herbs.
This flavour lasts even longer
on the palate when accompanied
by the vodka, while citrus fruits
enhance the partnership.**

1
Remove the zest from the lemon and orange, then
slice thinly. Fill a saucepan with 350 ml/12 fl oz
water. Add the honey and the citus slices and warm
over low heat.

2
Stir in the agar-agar, then bring to the boil. Remove
from the heat and let infuse for 10 minutes, then
remove the zests. Retain the zests for decoration.

3
In a bowl, combine the lemon juice and the vodka.
Add the honey mixture. Season with a few turns
of the peppermill.

4
Transfer to a sorbet machine and proceed according
to manufacturer's instructions. Serve decorated with
the citrus zests. If not serving immediately, transfer
to a freezer-proof container with a lid and freeze.

CHEF'S ADVICE
*Serve with caviar or smoked fish (best-quality salmon, trout, eel,
halibut or herring) accompanied by fried onions.*
*Agar-agar is an algae-based gelling agent. It can be replaced by
powdered gelatine.*

starters

Goat Cheese and Rhubarb Tarts
with Szechuan Pepper

**Preparation: 30 minutes
(3 hours in advance for
the rhubarb compote)
Cooking time: 30 minutes
Serves 4**

FOR THE TARTS
50 g/1 3/4 oz unsalted butter
8 filo pastry sheets
1 tablespoon whole Szechuan
peppercorns in a peppermill
4 Crottin de Chavignol
(goat's cheeses)
5 tablespoons olive oil
100 g/3 1/2 oz rocket
or mixed salad leaves
1 tablespoon sherry vinegar
Salt

FOR THE RHUBARB COMPOTE
300 g/11 oz rhubarb
125 g/4 oz sugar

Spice notes
**The creamy flavour of goat's cheese
brings out the camphorated,
woodsy qualities of the Szechuan
pepper. The rhubarb adds both
bite and smoothness. Other goat's
cheese can be used in place
of the Crottin de Chavignol;
it is also nice with blue cheeses.
Fresh figs, dusted with freshly
ground Szechuan pepper can be
substituted for the rhubarb.**

1
Prepare the rhubarb compote: Wash the rhubarb
stalks, then split in half and remove the fibrous strings.
Cut into small sticks and toss with the sugar in a bowl.
Let stand for 2 hours.

2
Place the rhubarb in a pan and cook over low heat
for 20 minutes, stirring occasionally, until thick.
Set aside to cool.

3
Prepare the tarts: Preheat the oven to 180° C/350° F.
Melt the butter. Using a pastry brush, paint each filo
sheet with the melted butter. Sprinkle 3/4 tablespoon
ground Szechuan pepper over all, then stack the sheets
in pairs. Bake for 3 minutes. Cut into 4 triangles.

4
Cut the goat's cheeses in half through the middle
(as if slicing a roll for a sandwich). Drizzle over
2 tablespoons olive oil and sprinkle with the remaining
Szechuan pepper.

5
To assemble, allow 4 filo triangles per person and put
the cheese halves on top. Spoon a dollop of rhubarb
compote on each and bake in the oven until the cheese
melts, about 5 minutes.

6
Toss the rocket leaves with the vinegar, remaining oil
and a pinch of salt and serve with the tarts.

CHEF'S ADVICE
*Frozen rhubarb pieces are an acceptable substitute for fresh; allow
250 g/9 oz. To use, add the sugar and then leave to defrost. This
compote will keep for up to ten days in the refrigerator.*

Scrambled Eggs
with Apple-Turmeric Chutney

Preparation: 45 minutes
Cooking time: 40 minutes
Serves 4

FOR THE EGGS
12 fresh eggs
Salt
40 g/1 1/2 oz unsalted butter
100 ml/3 1/2 fl oz crème fraîche
3/4 teaspoon poppy seeds

FOR THE APPLE CHUTNEY
1 onion
1 shallot
2 granny smith apples
50 g/ 1 3/4 oz unsalted butter
1 tablespoon acacia honey
50 ml/2 fl oz cider vinegar
1 teaspoon freshly grated ginger
3 pinches turmeric
2 pinches saffron
1 tablespoon prepared
American-style mustard

FOR THE SPICED OIL
2 garlic cloves
200 ml/7 fl oz olive oil
1 teaspoon thyme flowers
1/2 teaspoon piment d'Espelette
(or Cayenne pepper)

Spice notes
**Turmeric and saffron give
this chutney an elegant bitterness
mixed with a floral note,
enhanced by the peppery bite
of the ginger. Poppy seeds,
on the other hand, act as
a foil to mellow the flavours.
The chutney is equally delicious
with fish or poultry.**

1
Prepare the chutney: Peel and finely chop the shallot and onion. Peel the apples and cut into a dice. Place a knob of butter (about 10 g/1/4 oz) in a large pot over low heat. Add the shallot and onion and cook to soften. Add the rest of the butter, then the apples, honey, vinegar, ginger, turmeric and saffron. Stir and cook gently over low heat for 30 minutes.

2
When the chutney has softened, transfer to a bowl and stir in the mustard. Set aside to cool.

3
Prepare the spiced oil: Peel the garlic and place in a food processor. Add the oil, thyme and piment, and process. Let stand 15 minutes then strain and set aside.

4
Prepare the eggs: Break the eggs into a large bowl and beat lightly. Salt. Melt the butter in a heavy-bottomed pan. Add the eggs and cook, stirring constantly with a wooden spoon. As soon as they thicken, stir in the crème fraîche.

5
To serve, sprinkle the poppy seeds over the eggs and accompany with the spiced oil and chutney.

CHEF'S ADVICE
This recipe makes more chutney and spiced oil than is needed for one meal. Both will keep in the refrigerator for several days. This dish is perfect for a brunch, served with rashers of bacon.

Cold Curried Courgette Soup

Preparation: 20 minutes
(2 hours in advance)
Cooking time: 20 minutes
Serves 4

2 potatoes (about 200 g/7 oz)
1 leek, white part only
1 stick celery
2 garlic cloves
4–5 courgettes (about 1 kg/2 lb)
100 ml/3 1/2 fl oz olive oil
1 tablespoon mild curry powder
1 bouquet garni
(thyme, bay, parsley stems)
1 tomato
6 fresh basil leaves,
plus more for garnish
150 ml/1/4 pint
double cream, chilled
Whole white peppercorns
in a peppermill
Salt

)*Spice notes*
**Mild curry powder is made
from a blend of ten spices.
The dominant flavours come
from turmeric, coriander
and cumin, with a touch
of mustard; the floral notes
from aniseed and fennel make
it fresh and lively. Curry also
marries well with leek and
potato soup, or pumpkin soup.**

1

Peel the potatoes, then cut into cubes. Slice the leek lengthwise to expose the inner leaves and rinse under cold running water, then slice thinly. Wash the celery and cut into small pieces. Peel the garlic, then chop finely. Wash the courgettes, trim, then cut into cubes (do not peel).

2

Place 3 tablespoons olive oil in a large pot with the potatoes, leek, celery and garlic. Cook over low heat, without browning, until soft. Salt lightly and add 3/4 tablespoon of the curry powder. Stir vigorously, then add 1 more tablespoon olive oil and the courgettes. Stir well.

3

Add water just to cover. Bring to the boil, then add the bouquet garni and lower the heat. Simmer gently for 15 minutes, remove the bouquet garni. Strain, then purée the vegetables, adding as much of the cooking liquid as necessary to obtain a fluid consistency. (Bear in mind that you will be adding cream at the end as well, so not too liquid.) Refrigerate for 2 hours.

4

Seed the tomato, then cut into a fine dice. With a pair of scissors, snip 6 basil leaves into thin strips. Just before serving, gently whisk the cream into the soup.

5

To serve, ladle the soup into bowls. Garnish with the diced tomato and basil slivers. Dust each with the remaining curry powder and a few turns of the peppermill. Top with whole basil leaves, a drizzle of olive oil and serve.

CHEF'S ADVICE
There will be a thin layer of foam which rises to the surface as the soup boils. Skim it away before adding the bouquet garni.

Oyster Mushrooms
with Curry Vinaigrette

Preparation: 25 minutes
Cooking time: 15 minutes
Serves 4

FOR THE MUSHROOMS
800 g/1 3/4 lb oyster
mushrooms
1 small shallot
1 piece fresh ginger
30 g/1 oz cubed pancetta
2 pinches curry powder
Olive oil
Whole white Muntauk
peppercorns

FOR THE VINAIGRETTE
Leaves of 4 fresh
coriander stems
1 teaspoon Dijon mustard
1 tablespoon sherry vinegar
2 pinches medium
curry powder
Salt
4 tablespoons olive oil

Spice notes
**Clove and nutmeg mingle
to perfection in a medium curry
spice blend, and complement
the firey chilli and pepper tastes.
Herbal tones come from the
combination of onion, thyme,
bay and cumin. This marriage
of flavours works equally well
with most varieties of mushroom,
as a seasoning or a marinade. Try
ordinary mushrooms or shiitake.
Chanterelles have a more subtle
fruity taste and are better suited
to mild curry or anise.**

1
Prepare the mushrooms: Clean by rinsing briefly under running water; pat dry. Cut the large ones in half. Finely chop the shallot. Peel and grate the ginger to obtain about 1 teaspoon.

2
Brown the pancetta in a teflon pan. Remove from the pan and set aside. Pour some of the oil into the same pan. Add the mushrooms and cook over high heat until the cooking juices have evaporated and the mushrooms have browned.

3
Add salt to taste, then add the shallot, ginger, pancetta and curry. Stir gently. Season with three twists of the peppermill. Set aside.

4
Prepare the vinaigrette: Chop the coriander. Place the mustard in a small bowl. Add the vinegar and whisk to combine. Add 2 pinches of salt and the curry powder. Slowly pour in the oil, whisking constantly until blended.

5
Drizzle the vinaigrette over the mushrooms and sprinkle with the coriander. Add a few more twists of the peppermill and serve.

CHEF'S ADVICE
Serve with a mixed green salad. Poached eggs and a loaf of hearty rustic bread will turn this into a complete meal. As a change from traditional vegetables, serve these mushrooms with your next roast dinner.

Mango and Prawn Salad
with Spicy Ginger Vinaigrette

Preparation: 15 minutes
Serves 4

FOR THE SALAD
2 mangoes, slightly green
400 g/14 oz prawns
cooked in shells
8 fresh mint leaves

FOR THE VINAIGRETTE
1 5 cm/2 in piece
of fresh ginger
1 lemon
Salt
White Muntauk pepper
1/4 teaspoon ground chilli
1 tablespoon soy sauce
4 tablespoons pine oil
(see "Chef's advice"
for alternatives)

1
Prepare the salad: Peel the mangoes, slice and refrigerate until needed. Peel the prawns, keeping the tail fin intact for a more attractive presentation.

2
Prepare the vinaigrette: Grate the ginger to obtain about 1 tablespoon. Squeeze the lemon over a small bowl. Add salt, 2 pinches of pepper, chilli, soy sauce, ginger and oil and whisk to blend.

3
Combine the mangoes and prawns. Pour over the vinaigrette. Cut the mint leaves into thin strips and sprinkle over the salad. Serve.

CHEF'S ADVICE
Pine oil has a full and lightly charred flavour which blends perfectly with the freshness of the salad. As an alternative, make the vinaigrette using half hazelnut oil and half grapeseed oil.

Spice notes
Chilli can often interfere with other flavours because it is so strong; in this recipe it enhances the overall taste with its pleasant lingering fire. The Muntauk pepper is a sensual addition, adding bite to the freshness of the mango. Bracing ginger and mint round out the whole. This tropical mix of tastes will add swing to any gathering. Crab or langoustines are both suitable substitutes for the prawns.

overleaf
caraway seeds, mace

Tropical Island Scallops

Preparation: 15 minutes

Serves 4

FOR THE SCALLOPS

Tropical Island Seasoning
Salt
12 fresh scallops
1/2 lemon
2 tablespoons hazelnut oil
Brittany sea salt
(or fleur de sel)

FOR THE GARNISH

Small pansies or violets, and
a handful of lamb's lettuce

Spice notes

**Tropical Island Seasoning consists
of coriander seed, caraway,
oregano and white pepper and
it is the perfect foil for the silky
texture and salty taste of raw
scallops. The anise, pepper
and herbal, spicy scents evoke
the aroma of spice shops of
yesteryear, and of faraway islands.
Spice mixes need a good shake
before grinding to ensure
all the flavours mingle equally.
This mixture is also superb
with grilled whole small quids
or turbot fillets.**

1

Prepare the plates: Dust each with 3 grinds of the
peppermill and 3 pinches of salt.

2

Rinse the scallops under cold running water and pat
dry. Slice each into four thin rounds.

3

Arrange the scallop slices on the prepared plates.
Grind over some more pepper, about 3 twists
per plate. Lightly sprinkle with the sea salt and
squeeze fresh lemon juice over all (a few drops each).
Finish with a drizzle of oil.

4

Decorate with a scattering of flowers and the lamb's
lettuce.

CHEF'S ADVICE

*Serve with thick slices of toasted rustic bread. Do not use the orange
part of the scallops which have an unpleasant texture when raw,
though they are delicious sautéed in butter with lots of chopped
fresh parsley.*

John Dory Fillets
with Vanilla Oil and Pink Peppercorns

**Preparation: 20 minutes
(2 days in advance
for the vanilla oil)
Serves 4**

2 vanilla pods
150 ml/1/4 pint olive oil
350 g/12 oz very fresh fish
fillets, John Dory
or sea bream
Brittany sea salt
(or fleur de sel)
Whole pink peppercorns

) *Spice notes*
**Vanilla serves to heighten
the flavours in this dish instead
of the usual lemon juice. In
combination with the olive oil,
vanilla adds allure and bite,
whereas in sweet dishes
it adds subtlety. Be sure to use
a delicately scented olive oil,
with a slightly almondy taste;
those from the south of France
are good. The pink peppercorns
add tartness.**

1
Two days in advance, pour the oil into a bowl. Split the vanilla pods lengthwise down the middle and scrape the seeds into the bowl. Stir, cover and leave to marinate at room temperature.

2
The day of serving: Cut the fish fillets into thin slices. Sprinkle 4 plates with the sea salt. Arrange the fish on the plates and drizzle over the vanilla oil, then several twists of the peppermill. Decorate with a few whole peppercorns and a light sprinkling of the sea salt. Serve.

CHEF'S ADVICE
John Dory fillets are very delicate and easy to cut into thin slices. If using another type of fish, be sure to use a very sharp knife or ask the fishmonger to do it for you. This is a simple, easy to prepare recipe but the fish must be of the utmost freshness.

Smoked Salmon
with Herb-Spice Jacket Potatoes

Preparation: 30 minutes
Cooking time: 55 minutes
Serves 4

8 medium potatoes
6 tablespoons crème fraîche
Coarse ground black
peppercorns
20 g/3/4 oz unsalted butter
Whole nutmeg
Ground allspice
Half a bunch of fresh chives
Salt
350 g/12 oz finest
cold-smoked salmon fillets

Spice notes
**Nutmeg is the perfect partner
for potatoes, adding a hint
of woodsiness which is reinforced
by the clove and pepper of the
allspice. Salmon is at once fruity
and fatty, and with a lightly salty
flavour, it finds a home from
home on land in this dish.
Coarse peppercorns add bite
in place of lemon juice.**

I
Preheat the oven to 180° C/350° F. Wash and dry
the potatoes. Wrap in aluminium, place on a baking
tray and bake for 45 minutes. Remove and let cool.
Keep the oven on.

2
Bring the crème fraîche to the boil with the peppercorns. As soon as it boils, remove from the heat
and set aside.

3
Unwrap the potatoes. Using a spoon, scoop out
three-quarters from the centres and combine the
scooped out potatoes with the crème fraîche. Add
the butter, a grating of nutmeg, a pinch of allspice,
and the chives snipped with a scissors. Stir well.

4
Stuff the potato shells with the herb-spice potato
mixture and return to the oven for 5 minutes.

5
Slice the salmon into 4 pieces and place in the oven
for 2 minutes. Season lightly with a pinch of salt and
coarse peppercorns. Serve with the jacket potatoes.

CHEF'S ADVICE
*To keep the potatoes upright, slice a bit from the bottom, before
stuffing, to give them a flat base to sit on.*

Baked Truffles
with Muntauk Pepper

Preparation: 20 minutes
Cooking time: 30 minutes
Serves 4

300 ml/1/2 pint champagne
250 ml/9 fl oz chicken stock
350 ml/1/2 pint
crème fraîche
Brittany sea salt
(or fleur de sel)
Whole white Muntauk
peppercorns
1 carrot (about 120 g/3 1/2 oz)
40 g/1 1/2 oz piece of celeriac
2 shallots
50 g/1 3/4 oz unsalted butter
4 fresh truffles
(about 150-200g/5-7 oz),
brushed clean
250 g/9 oz prepared
puff pastry

Spice notes
**This is the climactic meeting of
two sensual and powerful aromas:
the lusty truffle and the savage
peppercorn. Champagne
and celeriac add sparkle.**

1
Combine the champagne and stock in a pan and cook
until reduced by half. Add the crème fraîche, a pinch
of sea salt and 3 twists of the peppermill. Continue
cooking until thick and slightly syrupy. You should
have about 425 ml/15 fl oz.

2
Meanwhile, peel the carrot and celeriac and cut both
into a small dice. Peel and finely chop the shallot.
Melt the butter in a pan. Add the carrot, celeriac
and shallot and cook for 2 minutes; they should
stay crunchy.

3
With an immersion mixer (or a blender) whisk
the champagne cream until frothy. Add the vegetables
and warm gently for 2 minutes. Divide the sauce
between 4 small gratin dishes or ramekins. Add
a truffle to each and set aside to cool.

4
Meanwhile, roll out the pastry and cut to 4 circles,
just slightly larger than the truffle containers. Place
1 pastry circle on top of each and pinch around
the edges to seal. Refrigerate for 20 minutes.

5
Preheat the oven to 180° C/350° F. Bake the truffles
for 20 minutes. Serve immediately, with a peppermill
and small dish of sea salt on the table.

CHEF'S ADVICE
*This is not an everyday dish, though it is quite simple to prepare. It
is not an economical dish either, though it can just as easily be made
with truffle slivers laid on top of a bed of thinly sliced, cooked new
potatoes, prepared in the same way. This can be made up to 1 day
in advance, which will improve the flavour. Heat briefly to serve.*

Foie Gras Terrine
with Szechuan Pepper

**Preparation: 30 minutes
(6 days in advance)
Cooking time: 40 minutes**

About 1 kg/2 lb foie gras
(2 livers)
6 tablespoons sweet wine,
such as Jurançon
1 teaspoon Szechuan
peppercorns
1 teaspoon ground
white pepper
15 g/1/2 oz salt
Pinch of sugar

) *Spice notes*
**In this recipe, Szechuan pepper
becomes a flower that explodes
into contrasting flavours.
The slightly lemony flavour
is dominant, and it sets off the
silky richness of the foie gras
to perfection. The sweet wine
adds a candied, dried fruit note,
making for a balanced mix of
flavours which linger pleasantly.**

1
Remove the livers from the refrigerator about
30 minutes before beginning so that they are at the
right temperature. Place, curve-side up, on a work
surface. Carefully separate the lobes to find the veins;
remove these with the tip of a small knife.

2
Place the livers in a shallow bowl or baking dish. Add
the wine. Grind the Szechuan peppercorns and mix
with the white pepper, salt and sugar. Rub this spice
mixture over the foie gras, cover with plastic wrap and
refrigerate for 4-6 hours.

3
Preheat the oven to 100° C/200° F. Arrange
the livers, squashing them in head to tail fashion,
in a ceramic terrine mould. The livers should fit
tightly. Cover and place in a water bath of cool
water. Cook for 40 minutes. Remove and let cool
at room temperature.

4
Cut out a piece of card or plastic food container
(like a large rectangular ice cream container) to the
shape of the inside of the terrine mould. Place on top
of the dish and weight (a large food tin is perfect).
Refrigerate for 12 hours. Remove the weight, turn
out and drain, then return to the refrigerator.

5
Wait 3-4 days before serving, with slices of toast.

CHEF'S ADVICE
*When removing the veins, leave any tiny ones; they are hard to get
out and you risk tearing up the liver if you try to remove them. If
you want to remove all traces of blood, soak in cold water with a
bit of milk and coarse salt for 3 hours. Any shape terrine will work;
a rectangular one is the most traditional, just be sure that the
livers are packed in tightly.*

peppers

black Tellichery peppercorns *Grown in southwestern India. Perfect with grilled or roasted meat. Also available ground.*

szechuan pepper *Berries from a Chinese prickly ash tree, grown in the south. Look for berries that are whole and without twigs. Use for foie gras, roast poultry and desserts.*

SPICY OR FLAVOURSOME, pepper is the punctuation for any dish it flavours. Pepper is one of the most essential spices in any cuisine and to do justice to this spice it cannot be spoken of in the singular. Peppers are many, from many places, in many shapes and with many sensual aromas: wood, sap, musk, anise, and lemon.

All peppercorns, whether black, white or green are the fruit of the tropical vine, *piper nigrum,* which grows wild in the forests of India, Asia, Indonesia, Malaysia and Brazil. Pepper represents half the world's consumption of spices and demand is always very high.

The pepper plant has slender, veined leaves. Its white flowers give way to green berries which eventually turn red. The berries are harvested before they ripen. As they dry, they shrivel and turn dark, becoming what we know

white peppercorns

Ripe berries which are dried after removing outer layers. Use to enhance exotic salad ingredients, shellfish, stews. Also available ground.

fresh unripe peppercorn bunches

These will gradually turn red. Harvested while green,
these are pickled in brine or vinegar.

dehydrated green peppercorns

Spicy, vegetal berries. Crush and use to season salads,
fish or duck breast.

as black peppercorns. The flavour is always spicy, but different regions produce peppercorns with distinctive flavours. Indian Tellichery pepper is mellow with woody aromas. Pepper from the Malaysian province of Sarawak is fiery on the palate with warming vegetal undertones.

For white peppercorns, the berries are left on the plant until ripe, then they are harvested and left to soak for several days to remove the outer layers. The finest white peppercorns are labelled "DW", which means double washed. Removing these layers removes much of the spiciness, so white peppercorns tend to be subtler, with a fruity, woody aroma. The flavour will always depend on where and how the peppers are grown. For example, white Muntauk pepper is one of the finest, with an aroma that is at once lively, musky and fruity.

Nowadays, peppercorns are the preference but in ancient Greece and Rome, *piper longum*, long pepper (also known as Indonesian pepper) was coveted. Resembling small, thin, grainy pinecones, long pepper has a heady aroma of flowers and tropical wood.

long pepper (Indonesian peppercorns)
Mellow and fiery berries with a firm texture. Use to stud roast pork and poultry or baked pineapple. Ground, serve with mixed berries.

Other varieties have peppery flavours though they are not part of the pepper family. Szechuan pepper, for example, comes from a Chinese variety of small prickly ash trees. These split open upon ripening and the small black grains are removed to release a delicate aroma of anise and lemon-scented wood. Pink pep-percorns are another "false" pepper, which come from South America. They are fruity, resinous and tart, and add a pretty visual effect when mixed with green, white and black peppercorns.

Peppers are often mixed with other spices: coriander seeds, allspice berries or dried lemon peel. Grinding these together from a peppermill will uplift most any savoury dish.

black peppercorns *The best are smooth, without any dust or broken bits. As with all spices, store in airtight containers in a cool dark place.*

pink peppercorns *From a tree native to South America, with a resinous flavour. Used to season raw fish and salad.*

mignonnette pepper *A mixture of coarse ground black and white peppercorns. Use for raw salmon and grilled meats.*

house blends

five-berry mixture *Black, white, green pep-percorns, coriander seed, allspice, pink peppercorns.*

three peppercorn blend *Green, white, black.*

whole lemon pepper *Pepper with 20% dried lemon peel.*

fish

Tuna Steaks
with Mustard and Fennel

Preparation: 20 minutes
Cooking time: 25 minutes
Serves 4

FOR THE TUNA
2 teaspoons caraway seed
2 teaspoons fennel seeds
3 tablespoons flour
6 tablespoons single cream
4 teaspoons mustard powder
4 tuna steaks
(about 150 g/5 oz each),
cut from the heart of the fillet
Olive oil
Brittany sea salt
(or fleur de sel)

FOR THE FENNEL SAUCE
1 fennel bulb
6 sprigs fresh dill
1 lime
6 tablespoons olive oil
Salt

Spice notes
**A summery dish in which caraway,
dill and fennel (which share
botanical heritage) add a note
of freshness, almost minty.
Mustard balances with its sharp
bite but also a hint of raisiny
sweetness which complements
the tuna. Salmon and trout can
also be used in this recipe.**

1
Prepare the tuna: Place the caraway and fennel seeds in a small teflon pan and cook briefly over high heat to toast the seeds. Remove and crush lightly. Divide the flour, cream and all the seeds between 3 separate plates.

2
Dip the tuna steaks first in the flour, the cream and then the seeds. Refrigerate until needed.

3
Meanwhile, prepare the fennel sauce: Trim and remove any bruised pieces from the fennel bulb. Cut into large pieces. Cook in boiling, salted water for 15 minutes, then drain.

4
Chop the dill and mix with the fennel keeping 1 dill sprig for garnish. Add the lime juice and the olive oil and season to taste.

5
Heat a few tablespoons of the olive oil in a pan and add the tuna steaks when hot. As soon as they are seared, lower the heat and cook 5 minutes per side. Sprinkle with the sea salt. Decorate with dill, and serve the fennel on the side.

CHEF'S ADVICE
Serve with boiled potatoes that have been coarsely mashed with olive oil. Cooking time for the tuna steaks will depend on their thickness. They do not need to be cooked all the way through, slightly pink will improve the overall flavour and keep them tender.

Sea Bream
with Clove and Hot Pepper Blend

Preparation: 30 minutes
(plus 4 hours marinating time)
Cooking time: 20 minutes
Serves 4

FOR THE FISH

2 large sea bream, 800 g/1 3/4
lb each, gutted and scaled
Olive oil
Brittany sea salt (or fleur de sel)
Hot Pepper Blend
4 rosemary sprigs
100 ml/ 3 1/2 fl oz dry white wine
100 ml/ 3 1/2 fl oz Noilly-Prat
(or vermouth)
100 ml/ 3 1/2 fl oz chicken stock
(or water)

FOR THE MARINADE

2 oranges
2 garlic cloves
3 cloves
60 g/2 1/4 oz honey
100 ml/ 3 1/2 fl oz soy sauce

Spice notes
**The clove and mixed peppercorns
add a slightly resinous flavour,
which is heightened by the citrus
flavours. These combine to give
the dish a festive holiday taste,
reminiscent of days spent fishing
or boating. Hot Pepper Blend is
the ideal seasoning for any grilled
fish. Add at the last minute to
maximise the flavour.**

I
Prepare the marinade: Zest the oranges and slice
thinly; squeeze the juice. Peel and crush the garlic
with the cloves. Combine the honey, soy sauce
and orange juice. Stir in half the orange zests,
and the garlic-clove mixture.

2
For the fish, rinse and pat dry. Make 3 short,
deep incisions in the flesh. Pour over the marinade.
Refrigerate for 4 hours, turning the fish once.

3
Preheat the oven to 200° C/400° F. Remove the fish
from the marinade and pat dry; reserve the marinade.
Drizzle some olive oil into a baking dish and sprinkle
lightly with sea salt. Place the fish on top, adding
more oil and salt on top. Give a few twists of the
peppermill and add 2 rosemary sprigs.

4
Bake the fish for 7 minutes. Add the wine and
the Noilly-Prat. Bake for a further 5 minutes.
Add the chicken stock and baste. Cook for a further
7-8 minutes, or until the fish are cooked through,
basting often.

5
Decorate with the remaining orange zests and the
rosemary and serve.

CHEF'S ADVICE
*Japanese soy sauce tends to have a richer flavour; Kikkoman is a
good brand. Taste the marinade before baking the fish; soy is salty
so it may only be necessary to salt before serving.*

Haddock Fillets
with Coconut-Tandoori Sauce

Preparation: 25 minutes
Cooking time: 15 minutes
Serves 4

1 garlic clove
6 sprigs coriander
2 small limes
5 large tomatoes
Whole coriander seeds
in a peppermill
2 tablespoons tandoori
spice mix
200 ml/ 7 fl oz coconut milk
4 haddock fillets,
about 125 g/4 oz each
1 tablespoon flour
Olive oil
Salt

Spice notes
**The sweetness of the coconut
enhances the woodsy, spicy, floral
and slightly anise flavour of
the tandoori spices. Coriander
and lime are the perfect foil,
adding a hint of freshness to calm
the fire of the spice. This is a
fast and easy way to bring a taste
of India to your table. Any kind
of white fish fillet can be used:
cod, halibut, etc; it is also
delicious with pork tenderloin,
lamb and chicken breasts.**

1
Peel and chop the garlic. Finely chop the fresh coriander. Squeeze the juice of 1 lime. Plunge the tomatoes into boiling water for 10 seconds, then transfer to cold water. Peel, seed and chop the tomatoes. Mix them with the garlic, coriander and lime juice. Salt lightly and give three grinds of the coriander seed.

2
Combine 1 tablespoon of the tandoori spice and the coconut milk in a pan. Cook over moderate heat for 10 minutes. Add the juice from the remaining lime.

3
Put the flour in a plate. Rinse and dry the fish fillets, then dip in the flour to coat lightly. Season with salt and the remaining tandoori spice mix.

4
Pour a small amount of oil into a teflon pan. Cook the fillets about 2 minutes each side. Serve with the coconut sauce poured over each fillet and the tomato salad on the side.

CHEF'S ADVICE
Be sure to shake the coconut milk well before opening as it has a tendency to separate.

Salmon Two Ways
with Mixed Peppercorns

**Preparation: 25 minutes
(1 hour in advance for
the marinade)
Cooking time: 5 minutes
Serves 4**

4 salmon steaks, about
150 g/5 oz each
2 sprigs thyme
Olive oil
Five-Berry Mixture
1 tomato
1 cucumber
1 celery heart, finely chopped
125 g/4 oz salmon fillet
Juice of 1 lime
Salt
1/2 bunch chives,
finely chopped
1/2 bunch coriander,
finely chopped
1 teaspoon capers

1
Place the salmon steaks in a dish. Add the leaves of 1 thyme sprig. Drizzle with 2 tablespoons olive oil and add a few grinds of the peppermill. Marinate in the refrigerator for 1 hour.

2
Rinse and seed the tomato. Peel the cucumber. Cut both into a fine dice of equal size. Mix with 1 tablespoon of the chopped celery. Chop the salmon fillet into a small dice.

3
Combine the diced salmon and vegetables. Add the remaining thyme leaves, a drizzle of oil and 1 teaspoon lime juice. Season with salt and a few grinds of the peppermill. Stir in the chives and coriander. Set aside.

4
Remove the salmon steaks from the marinade and pat dry. Cook in a teflon pan over high heat for 2 minutes each side. Salt and pour over the rest of the lime juice and a sprinkling of water. Sprinkle over the capers and serve with the salmon tartare.

Spice notes
The green and pink peppercorns in the spice mix add a touch of Scandinavian freshness, which is ideal for the fattiness of the salmon. A note of spicy warmth from the white and black peppercorns, and the allspice, balances the mix. Five-Berry Mixture is a delicious seasoning alternative to ordinary pepper. We especially recommend it for use with raw fish dishes.

CHEF'S ADVICE
Use the finest, freshest salmon available, generally Scottish or Norwegian as their farming and feeding conditions are regulated by a governing body.

overleaf
dill, turmeric

Shellfish
with Curry and Lemongrass

Preparation: 20 minutes
(2 hours in advance
for the cockles and clams)
Cooking time: 10 minutes
Serves 4

2 1/2 kg/5 lb fresh shellfish
(mussels, cockles, clams)
1 lime
200 ml/7 fl oz dry white wine
1 teaspoon mild curry powder
2 pinches ground chilli
4 salad onions, white and
green parts chopped
and kept separate
1 garlic clove, crushed
1 teaspoon dried lemongrass
1 teaspoon fresh grated ginger
150 ml/5 1/2 fl oz
coconut milk

1
Soak the cockles and clams in cold salted water for 2 hours, changing the water several times, to remove the sand.

2
Clean the mussels. Remove the lime zest and squeeze the juice. Put in a large pan and add the wine, curry, chilli, garlic, lemongrass, ginger and white onions.

3
Bring the wine mixture to the boil for 3 minutes, add the drained shellfish and remove them as they open, about 7 minutes.

4
Arrange the shellfish on a serving plate with the green onion slices scattered on top. Strain the cooking liquid into another pan and add the coconut milk. Bring to the boil and pour immediately over the shellfish. Toss and serve.

Spice notes
Chilli and ginger add fire, which is softened by the floral notes of the mild curry powder. Lemongrass stimulates the sensations. Coconut milk serves to temper the mixture and link the spices in a celebration of authentic seaside flavours. If you dare, try this with oysters, lightly poached in the spiced wine and coated with the coconut sauce.

CHEF'S ADVICE
To heighten the complexity of flavours, reduce the wine mixture to three-quarters. The shellfish will give off liquid during cooking which will fill out the mixture.

Peppered Scallops in their Shells

Preparation: 25 minutes
Cooking time: 15 minutes
Serves 4

20 scallops, with 4 shells
2 medium onions
2 shallots
3 garlic cloves
100 g/3 1/2 oz salted butter
Fine Brittany sea salt
Ground white pepper
200 ml/7 fl oz muscadet
4 tablespoons coarse fresh
white breadcrumbs
1 bunch fresh flat-leaf parsley
2 tablespoons dried
breadcrumbs

Spice notes
**White pepper is a classic spice
and absolutely essential here.
It adds just the right amount
of bite and, with its full flavour,
is the perfect partner for seafood.
Try it also with a gratin of fennel,
of courgettes or potatoes.**

1
Rinse the scallop shells and set aside. Slice each scallop into 4-6 cubes.

2
Peel and chop the onions, shallots and garlic. Heat in a pan with 30 g/ 1 oz butter until soft but not browned. Add the scallops, with a pinch of salt and a generous pinch of pepper. Raise the heat and cook, stirring constantly, for 30 seconds. Remove the scallops with a slotted spoon.

3
Add the wine to the liquid in the pan and cook over high heat until reduced by half, about 2 minutes. Add pepper, return the scallops to the pan and add the fresh breadcrumbs and the parsley. Stir, then divide this mixture between the scallop shells.

4
Melt the remaining butter until it just browns. Pour over the scallops and sprinkle with the dried breadcrumbs. Run under the grill to brown for 3-4 minutes. Serve immediately.

CHEF'S ADVICE
This is a traditional recipe from Brittany, which also calls for the white part around the scallop, or gills. If you decide to use them, be sure to rinse well because they are often quite sandy. To keep the shells stable on the plates, set them on top of seaweed or coarse salt.

Sesame Sea Bass
with Vegetable Couscous

Preparation: 30 minutes
Cooking time: 1 hour 10 minutes
(1 hour for the vegetable broth)
Serves 4

FOR THE FISH
4 sea bass fillets with skin,
about 150 g/5 oz each
2 tablespoons olive oil
2 tablespoons sesame seeds
Salt

FOR THE COUSCOUS
2 carrots
1 onion
1 courgette
1 red pepper
1 celery stalk
4 tomatoes
Salt
Ground chilli
250 g/9 oz couscous
2 tablespoons olive oil
30 g/1 oz unsalted butter

1
Prepare the couscous broth: Wash all the vegetables. Peel the carrots and onion. Cut all the vegetables into a small dice. Place in a large stockpot, add water to cover, salt and cook, covered, over low heat for 1 hour. Add a pinch of chilli.

2
Prepare the couscous according to the instructions on the packet, adding some olive oil to the cooking liquid. With a fork, stir in the butter, fluffing the grains. Set aside.

3
Make small incisions in the skin to keep the fillets from shrinking during cooking. Season with salt. Heat some olive oil in a pan and cook the fillets, skin-side down, for 1 minute. Lower the heat and cook for a further 6-7 minutes.

4
Toast the sesame seeds in a teflon pan. Serve the fish fillets on a bed of couscous and sprinkle over the sesame seeds. Serve the vegetable broth on the side.

Spice notes
Searing the fish skin intensifies the flavour, which is enhanced by the toasted sesame seeds. The lightly spiced couscous will transport you on a voyage through the flavours of North Africa. Toasted sesame seeds can be sprinkled on any number of dishes to add a pleasant nutty, grilled taste. Try them on quail, a leg of lamb or honey-roasted chicken.

CHEF'S ADVICE
This is a cheat's version of fish couscous, which is even more delicious when made with shellfish as well. The vegetable broth should be flavoursome; do not add too much water.

Langoustines
with Chanterelles and Seven Spices

Preparation: 35 minutes
Cooking time: 10-12 minutes
Serves 4

FOR THE LANGOUSTINES
16 langoustines
800 g/1 3/4 lb chanterelle
mushrooms
1 shallot
8 walnuts
Salt
Grapeseed oil
1 bunch chives, snipped
with scissors

FOR THE SPICE MIX
10 cardamom pods
1 teaspoon whole white
Muntauk peppercorns
2 teaspoons whole
coriander seeds
1 teaspoon Szechuan pepper
1 teaspoon anise seeds
1 teaspoon ground turmeric
1 vanilla pod

Spice notes
**This Fauchon spice combination
is fruity and intensely woodsy.
It is ideal with the slightly salty-
sweet taste of the langoustines.
Cardamom lends a hint of
resinous, lemony taste that
reminds of exotic seaside holidays,
while the anise-like tartness of
the Szechuan pepper complements
the chanterelles. Muntauk pepper
and vanilla make the whole mix
sing. This spice mixture can be
made in advance and stored in
an airtight container.**

1
Prepare the spice mix: Remove the cardamom seeds from the papery pods and place in a peppermill with the Muntauk pepper, coriander, Szechuan pepper and anise seeds. Grind to a powder. Stir in the turmeric and black vanilla beans which have been scraped from the pod.

2
Coat the langoustines with the spice mix (leave a bit for the chanterelles).

3
Wash the mushrooms by quickly rinsing under cold, running water; they should not be soaked. Peel and chop the shallot. Shell the walnuts.

4
Put the mushrooms in a large teflon pan. Season, cover and cook for 5 minutes. Strain.

5
Return the mushrooms to the pan and stir in 2 tablespoons oil. Cook over high heat for about 3 minutes; they should retain some crunch. Add the shallot and walnuts. Season with salt and 2 pinches of the spice mix.

6
Cook the langoustines in a hot pan with 2 tablespoons of oil, stirring constantly, for 3 minutes. Salt and stir in the chives. Serve with the chanterelles.

CHEF'S ADVICE
If preparing this with fresh walnuts in season, be sure to remove the inner skin which is bitter. The neutral taste of grapeseed oil is ideal here as it does not interfere with the other flavours in the dish. You can add a few drops of walnut oil just before serving which will intensify the nutty taste, but don't overdo it.

Grilled Lobster
with Sarawak Pepper

Preparation: 25 minutes
Cooking time: 12-15 minutes
Serves 4

2 large Brittany lobsters,
about 500 g/18 oz each
Coarse sea salt
2 teaspoons whole black
Sarawak peppercorns
8 branches fresh coriander
1 large orange
2 large shallots
70 g/2 1/2 oz unsalted butter
1 tablespoon crème fraîche

Spice notes
**The full glory of Sarawak pepper
is brought out in this dish,
where its lingering, raw flavour
contrasts with the delicate
firm lobster flesh. A cheat's recipe
is to simply prepare the lobsters,
dot with butter and run under
a very hot grill. Season with salt
and Sarawak pepper and serve.**

1
Bring 3 litres/5 1/2 pints water to the boil with a large
handful of salt. Cook the lobsters for 2 minutes.
Drain and let cool. Grind the peppercorns. Chop
half the coriander.

2
Remove the claws, break the shell to extract the meat.
Slice the lobsters in half from head to tail. Remove
the sandy bits from a sort of pouch you will find
near the head. Remove the coral and creamy parts
and retain for later. Wipe all the empty cavities dry
and fill with claw meat. Season the flesh with
salt and pepper.

3
Remove the zest from the orange and slice thinly.
Squeeze the juice. Peel and chop the shallots.
Cook the shallots in 20 g/3/4 oz of the butter until
soft. Add the orange juice and reduce over high
heat, gradually incorporating the rest of the butter.
Stir in the crème fraîche.

4
Stir in half the coriander leaves. Add the reserved
coral and other bits. Sprinkle with pepper. Arrange
the lobster halves in a baking dish.

5
Pour the sauce over the lobster flesh and let it pool
in the empty cavities. Run under the grill for
3-5 minutes; the time will depend on the size of the
lobster. Garnish with the rest of the coriander and
the orange zests. Pepper again and serve.

CHEF'S ADVICE
*Brittany lobsters have the finest flavour and are recommended
for this dish. It can be made with lobster from any origin, and
some (especially Canadian lobster) are even better when you add
2 tablespoons armagnac or whisky to the orange sauce.*

anise-scented and herbaceous spices

star anise, or badian anise *Fruit of the badian tree, forms an 8-pointed star-shaped pod. Use in fruit and vegetables compotes, jams, chutneys and vinegars.*

fennel seed *Use to season shellfish, fish and vegetables. Also available ground.*

ANISE, STAR ANISE, FENNEL, CARAWAY, CUMIN AND CORIANDER all share a common aroma. They have a scent of anise and a fresh flavour, which is sometimes tinged with bitterness. All these spices come from plants which bear parasol-shaped flowers, except star anise which comes from a small tree. Caraway comes from India, and Northern and Eastern Europe, where it is used to season cheese, such as munster, as well as pastries. It has certain medicinal properties, as does cumin, whose distinctive aroma fills the air on market days in Northern Africa, Iran, Turkey, South America and India. Cumin's full-bodied flavour enhances chillies, curry and tandoori blends, as well as the heady Moroccan ras-el-hanout spice mixture. Coriander seeds, also a common ingredient in these spice blends, have a smooth, orange peel aroma. These are delicious in marinades, sprinkled over scallops and in the company of caraway seed, peppercorns and oregano, as in Tropical Island Seasoning. The small seeds hidden inside the pods of a star anise are not as aromatic as the pods themselves. These contain anethol, which is the same essential oil found in anise.

caraway seed *Aroma of anise and eucalyptus. Delicious with fish soups.*

celery seed *With a punchy, bitter taste, use to add flavour to court bouillon, in combination with salt and tomato-based dishes.*

coriander seed *Delicate, use whole in Mediterranean-style marinades. Or grind and use with shellfish.*

cumin *Whole and ground, it is slightly bitter and peppery. Use to season lamb, carrots and cheese.*

ras-el-hanout *Coriander, turmeric, cumin, caraway, chilli, salt.*

tandoori seasoning blend *Turmeric, cumin, mustard seed, anise, fenugreek, fennel seed, clove, chilli.*

house blends

Cod with Chorizo

and Piment d'Espelette

Preparation: 35 minutes
Cooking time: 50 minutes
(of which 10 for the fish)
Serves 4

1 red pepper
1 green pepper
2 long sweet peppers
3 onions
2 garlic cloves
4 large, ripe tomatoes
Olive oil
Ground black pepper
Salt
Piment d'Espelette
(or Ground Cayenne Pepper)
4 thick cod fillets, about
200 g/7 oz each
8 slices chorizo
50 g/1 3/4 oz Bayonne ham
trimmings
(or Parma ham)
1 small bunch
flat-leaf parsley, chopped

Spice notes
**Piment d'Espelette comes from
the south-western Basque region
of France and has a sweet,
slightly fruity flavour very similar
to that of a Spanish pimiento.
It explodes into a galaxy of sunny
peppery flavours on the palate.
A few pinches will add heavenly
fire to sautéed prawns, stuffed
calamari or spaghetti tossed
with olive oil and roasted garlic.**

1
Prepare the pepper sauce: Cut open the peppers
and remove the white veins and seeds, then slice.
Peel and chop the onions and garlic. Peel, seed and
chop the tomatoes.

2
In a shallow pan, cook the peppers in 4 tablespoons
oil for 5 minutes. Add the onion, garlic and
tomatoes. Season with salt and pepper and a few
pinches of Cayenne. Cover and let cook over low
heat for 30 minutes.

3
Preheat the oven to 200° C/400° F. Slice the chorizo
into sticks. Make several incisions in the cod fillets
and fill with the chorizo slivers. Sprinkle with
Cayenne pepper. Roll up the fillets and fasten with
kitchen string.

4
Arrange the cod rolls in a baking dish and drizzle
with oil, salt and pepper. Bake for 10 minutes.

5
Quickly fry the ham, then add to the pepper sauce.
Sprinkle the cod with the parsley and serve straight
away, with the pepper sauce.

CHEF'S ADVICE
*This can also be made with very thick cod fillets, with the skin.
In this case, cook skin-side down. For a truly authentic Basque
taste, add some sautéed small squid. Long, thin green peppers are
easily found in the Basque region of France and their flavour is
more delicate than that of an ordinary green pepper. If long
peppers are unavailable, you can use green pepper instead.*

Fish with Island Fruit
and Cayenne Pepper

**Preparation: 20 minutes
(3 hours marinating time)
Cooking time: 5 minutes
Serves 4**

200 ml/7 fl oz coconut milk
2 limes
1 small bunch chives,
snipped with scissors
1 piece fresh ginger
Whole white Muntauk
peppercorns
Ground Cayenne pepper
4 tomatoes
2 small mangoes
1 papaya
4 jobfish fillets, about
180 g /6 1/2 oz each
(or use snapper,
sea bream or porgy)
Olive oil
Salt
4 banana leaves, for wrapping

Spice notes

**The aromas of Cayenne, ginger
and pepper which are released
when the wrapping is open will
transport you to a faraway tropical
land. The mingling of fish
and fruit is enhanced and
enriched by the Muntauk pepper.
Try these same spices with
grouper, monkfish or other
unusual fish from warm waters.**

1
Warm the coconut milk in a pan. Add the juice
of 1 lime, half the chives, 1 tablespoon grated ginger,
2 good twists of the peppermill, and a knifepoint-
full of Cayenne. Pour this over the fish and marinate
for 3 hours.

2
Peel, seed and cut the tomatoes into a dice. Cut
the mango into cubes (without the skin). Halve the
papaya, scrape out the seeds and cut into cubes.

3
Drain the fish fillets (reserve the marinade) and
season with salt. Wrap each in a banana leaf. Steam
for 5 minutes.

4
Add the fruit to the marinade, with a drizzle of oil,
a pinch of Cayenne and salt. Squeeze the remaining
lime juice over the fish fillets, decorate with chives
and serve with the sauce.

CHEF'S ADVICE
*Banana leaves can be found in Oriental speciality shops, or you
can use baking parchment. Jobfish is found in the Seychelles. It
has a firm flesh which is ideal for raw-cooking, similar to the
method used here with the lime juice-coconut marinade. Be sure
not to over-steam.*

Red Mullet
with Saffron Tomato Sauce

Preparation: 25 minutes
(30 minutes for the marinade)
Cooking time: 40 minutes
(4-5 minutes for the fish)
Serves 4

8 small red mullets, about
125 g/4 oz each, scaled
Ground white pepper
Olive oil
2 onions
2 shallots
2 garlic cloves
150 ml/ 5 1/2 fl oz dry
white wine
800 g/1 3/4 lb tomatoes
1 sachet of saffron threads
1 bouquet garni
1 organic, unwaxed lemon
1 bunch basil
Salt

Spice notes

The floral combination of slowly cooked tomato and saffron complements the strong flavour of the fish. Red mullet and saffron are paired in many Mediterranean dishes as the flavours have a natural affinity. Just like ceviche, it can be served cold, which softens the citrus flavours and enhances the saffron. Try with other fish: gurnard, scorpion fish or monkfish; either prepared as above or simply drizzled with olive oil and sprinkled with saffron before roasting.

1
Place the fish in a dish and season with pepper and a drizzle of oil. Refrigerate while you prepare the sauce.

2
Peel the onions and shallots and slice into thin rounds. Peel and crush the garlic. Peel, seed and finely chop the tomatoes.

3
In a large pot, cook the onions, shallots and garlic in 4 tablespoons oil until soft. Add the wine and bring to the boil. Let cook until reduced slightly, then add the tomatoes and three-quarters of the saffron. Season with salt and pepper and add the bouquet garni. Simmer gently for 25 minutes.

4
Preheat the oven to 200° C/400° F. Wash the lemon and cut into 8 thin slices. Pour the tomato sauce into a ceramic baking dish. Arrange the fish on top and pour over the marinating oil. Season with salt and pepper and top each with a lemon round.

5
Bake for 5-6 minutes. Remove from the oven and add the remaining saffron. With scissors, slice the basil leaves and sprinkle over the top. Let stand for several minutes, then serve.

CHEF'S ADVICE
Use a bouquet garni made from thyme, bay and basil stems. Red mullets do not need to be gutted.

Peppered Monkfish
with Spring Vegetables

Preparation: 45 minutes
Cooking time: 40 minutes
Serves 4

FOR THE MONKFISH AND VEGETABLES
4 thick pieces monkfish,
about 200 g/7 oz each
Salt
Mixed whole green,
white and black peppercorns
4 medium courgettes
8 thin carrots with tops
200 g/ 7 oz fine green beans
8 asparagus spears
150 g/5 oz fresh shelled beans

FOR THE SAUCE
1 bunch chervil
1 bunch chives
1 bunch tarragon
200 g/7 oz plain fromage frais
3 tablespoons mascarpone
Salt
Vinegar
Olive oil

Spice notes
**Green, white and black represent
all the stages of a peppercorn.
White peppercorns are the ripest
and lend a musky flavour; unripe
green peppercorns add a hint of
vegetal freshness, while black
peppercorns add spice. Together
they have a predominantly fresh
vegetal taste, in keeping with the
spring vegetables and enhancing
the flavour of the fish. A thick
rumpsteak can also be seasoned
in the same way before grilling.**

1
Prepare the sauce: Snip all the herbs with scissors.
Whisk together the fromage frais and mascarpone,
then stir in 2 tablespoons of each herb. Stir in some
salt, 1 teaspoon vinegar and a drizzle of oil.
Refrigerate.

2
Salt the fish fillets. Place the peppers in a mill
and grind over a plate in a layer. Put the fish on top
and roll around in the pepper to coat. Refrigerate.

3
Wash the vegetables. If the courgettes are thin, leave
them whole but peel the skin in alternating stripes.
If the courgettes are thicker, cut into long quarters.
Peel the carrots, leaving a bit of the green at the top.
Trim the green beans. Snap the asparagus tips.

4
Plunge the beans into boiling water for 10 seconds,
then cool. Push them between your fingertips so
they pop out of their skins.

5
Steam the vegetables separately: carrots for 12 minutes,
asparagus 8–10 minutes, courgettes, 6–8 minutes
(or 3-4 minutes for quarters), green beans for
5 minutes. Use stacking steamer baskets if you have
them and remove each layer as it cooks.

6
Steam the monkfish for 8 minutes. Arrange the fish
and vegetables on a platter and serve with the sauce.

CHEF'S ADVICE
*Change the vegetables according to season. You can also make this
with baby fennel bulbs, artichokes, peas, broccoli, small turnips.
If you do not have steamer baskets, cook the vegetables in salted,
boiling water until al dente. Be sure to refresh immediately in cold
water to stop the cooking and retain the crunch.*

Roast Turbot in Turmeric Broth

Preparation: 30 minutes
Cooking time: 40 minutes
(of which 10 for the fish)
Serves 4

FOR THE FISH AND RAVIOLI
4 turbot steaks,
about 180 g/6 1/2 oz each
Brittany sea salt
(or fleur de sel)
Whole Szechuan peppercorns
100 g/ 3 1/2 oz
salted butter
300 g/11 oz fresh ravioli

FOR THE BROTH
1 large carrot
1 leek, white part only
1/2 fennel bulb
1 celery heart
1 onion
1 clove
Salt
1 small bouquet garni
1 teaspoon whole
Szechuan peppercorns
1/2 teaspoon ground turmeric

Spice notes

The astringency of the Szechuan pepper and the freshness of the anise (fennel) create tension in the flavours. The whole is tempered by the gently lingering wildflower perfume of the turmeric and its golden colour. Turbot is a meaty fish with mild flavour that is greatly enhanced by this delicious, slightly exotic, broth. Try this recipe with skate wing or monkfish.

1
Prepare the broth: peel and chop the carrot. Wash the leek white, fennel, and celery and chop finely. Peel the onion and stud with the clove. Bring 1 litre/1 3/4 pints salted water to the boil. Add all the vegetables, and the bouquet garni and cook for 20 minutes. Strain, reserving the vegetables.

2
Add the Szechuan peppers and three-quarters of the turmeric to the broth and reduce to obtain about 300 ml/ 1 /2 pint.

3
Preheat the oven to 180° C/350° F. Season the fish with sea salt and several grinds of Szechuan pepper. Sprinkle over the remaining turmeric.

4
Brown the fish in a pan with the butter, 3 minutes on the first side, 2 minutes on the other. Transfer to a baking dish and roast for 5 minutes, basting with the broth.

5
Meanwhile, cook the ravioli according to packet instructions. Drain.

6
Serve the turbot with the broth and ravioli. You can use the reserved broth vegetables and celery leaves for decoration.

CHEF'S ADVICE
Warm the vegetables in the broth before serving. Lightly toast the Szechuan peppercorns before grinding to minimise bitterness. Ricotta-filled ravioli work best for this recipe.

meat

Roast Lamb
with Harissa

Preparation: 20 minutes
Cooking time: 20 minutes
Serves 4

FOR THE LAMB
2 garlic cloves
6 sprigs mint
6 sprigs coriander
Juice of 1 lime
2 teaspoons honey
2 teaspoons tomato purée
2 teaspoons Harissa spice mix
Olive oil
2 racks of lamb, about 8 ribs each
Salt

FOR THE COUSCOUS
200 g/7 oz couscous
1 tablespoon olive oil
50 g/1 3/4 oz unsalted butter
2 tablespoons almonds
12 grapes

Spice notes
Harissa is a mixture of ground peppers and chillies, coriander and dried garlic. It is very strong and spicy but can be tamed when paired with the freshness of herbs and citrus fruit. The aromas of honey, mint and coriander from the roasting lamb will transport you to a Moroccan souk.

1
Preheat the oven to 240° C/475° F. Finely chop the garlic. Strip the mint and coriander leaves from the stems and snip the leaves with scissors. Mix the lime juice with the honey. Stir in the garlic, herbs, tomato purée, harissa and 4 tablespoons oil.

2
Put the lamb racks in a roasting dish. Season with salt and pepper and drizzle with olive oil. Roast for 15 minutes. Remove from the oven and let stand 10 minutes.

3
Meanwhile, prepare the couscous according to packet instructions, adding the olive oil to the cooking liquid. After standing add three quarters of the butter, stirring with a fork to fluff the grains. Set aside.

4
Spread half the harissa mixture over the lamb. Roast for 5 minutes.

5
Dry-roast the almonds in teflon pan. Remove from the pan and add the grapes and the rest of the butter and cook until golden. Stir the almonds and grapes into the couscous.

6
Slice the lamb racks. Serve with the couscous and the remaining harissa mixture.

CHEF'S ADVICE
The flavour of the grapes will be better if they are peeled.
For a richer flavour, cook the butter until it browns before stirring into the couscous.

Chicken Tajine
with Lemon Spices

Preparation: 35 minutes
Cooking time: 1 hour 25 minutes
Serves 4-6

FOR THE CHICKEN
3 garlic cloves
100 ml/3 1/2 fl oz olive oil
1 large onion
2 preserved lemons (see page 130)
1 free-range chicken,
about 2 kg/4 1/2 lb, jointed
Salt
12 small olives (green or black)
1/2 bunch coriander
5 parsley stalks

FOR THE SPICES
1 teaspoon turmeric
1/2 teaspoon cumin seeds
1/2 teaspoon ground cinnamon
1 teaspoon ground ginger
Lemon Pepper blend

1
Prepare the spices: Put the spices in a small bowl and add 3 pinches Lemon Pepper. Set aside.

2
Peel and crush the garlic and mix with half of the oil. Peel the onion and chop. Remove the peel from half of a preserved lemon and cut into a small dice. Preheat the oven to 180° C/350° F.

3
Put the remaining oil in a large ovenproof pot with a lid. Add the onion and cook for 5 minutes. Add the chicken joints and cook for 5 minutes without browning. Stir in the spice mix, the garlic oil and the diced preserved lemon. Stir to blend and add some salt.

4
Add water to cover the chicken, put the lid on and bake for 1 hour. Add the olives and the remaining lemons, cut in quarters. Cook for a further 15 minutes. Degrease the cooking liquid. Chop the coriander and parsley leaves and stir in. Serve.

Spice notes
All the lemony aromas are gentle, but the pepper shows its strength and is supported by the ginger. This has a lively, slightly bitter taste which goes well with poultry. Turmeric and cinnamon add smoothness and combine with the aroma of coriander to affirme the North African inspiration in this dish.

CHEF'S ADVICE
You can add almonds for extra crunch.
This Moroccan dish takes its name from the cooking vessel, a tajine, which is a flat ceramic dish topped with a cone-shaped lid. This shape allows the steam to rise and fall, adding continuous moisture to whatever cooks inside. A pot with a lid that has a depression in it for adding water will produce a similar effect.
This can be made one day in advance and reheated before serving.

Foie Gras with Honey
and Lemon Pepper

Preparation: 10 minutes
(1 hour marinating time)
Cooking time: 15 minutes
Serves 4

1 foie gras weighing about
450 g/1 lb, sliced
Lemon Pepper blend
1 small unwaxed
organic orange
100 ml/3 1/2 fl oz vinegar
3 tablespoons acacia honey
1 star anise
1 cardamom pod
2 Granny Smith apples
40 g/ 1 1/2 oz unsalted butter
Salt

Spice notes
**Black Tellichery pepper has
a superb aroma of polished wood
and, in contact with the dried
lemon peel, it becomes both
fiery and vegetal. This is further
enhanced by the intense pine
and citrus flavour of the
cardamom. Anise adds a light
lingering floral sensation.**

1
Arrange the sliced liver in a dish which is big enough
for the pieces to fit without touching. Sprinkle with
3 pinches of Lemon Pepper. Cover with plastic wrap
and refrigerate for 1 hour.

2
Remove the orange part of the orange peel, taking
care not to get any white pith which is bitter. Slice
into long thin strips and blanch in boiling water for
1 minute. In a pot, combine the vinegar, orange
strips, honey, star anise, cardamom and 10 pinches
Lemon Pepper. Bring to the boil, then remove from
the heat. Let stand 1 hour, then strain, leaving some
orange strips for garnish.

3
Quarter and seed the apples. Cook in butter for
10 minutes, turning once. Set aside.

4
To serve, separately reheat the apples and spiced
vinegar. Salt the liver slices and cook in a teflon
pan for 30 seconds each side. Discard any cooking
juices. Drizzle the sauce over the liver and serve
with the apples.

CHEF'S ADVICE
*Prepared foie gras slices can sometimes be found in speciality shops,
in vacuum-packed bags. If you have a whole, fresh foie gras, follow
preparation instructions for the Foie Gras Terrine (see page 44).
Be sure to discard the cooking juices before pouring over the sauce.*

Veal Knuckle Blanquette
with Muntauk Pepper

Preparation: 45 minutes
Cooking time: 1 hour and
40 minutes
Serves 4

1 kg/2 lb 3 oz veal knuckle,
cut in pieces
2 carrots
2 leek whites
1 onion
2 cloves
1 garlic clove, peeled
1 small celery stick with leaves
Coarse salt
200 g/7 oz cup mushrooms
Juice of 1/2 lemon
150 g/5 oz pickling onions
100 g/3 1/2 oz unsalted butter
Whole white Muntauk
peppercorns
Ground nutmeg
2 egg yolks
200 ml/7 fl oz single cream

Spice notes
**This classic and well-loved
blanquette is brought up-to-date
with the addition of Muntauk
pepper which gives it a sensual
aroma to harmonise with
the melting texture of the veal.
The nutmeg added just before
serving adds a note of exotic
woodsiness, enhanced by the
creaminess of the sauce. You
will experience the same taste
sensations with chicken or fish.**

1
Put the veal in a large pot and add cold water to cover. Bring to the boil and skim off any foam that rises to the surface. Meanwhile, peel or wash the vegetables and add to the pot as you prepare them: chop the carrots and leeks, stud the onion with the cloves and add whole, with the garlic and celery. Add salt, cover and cook over low heat for 1 1/2 hours.

2
Rinse and trim the mushrooms. Combine with the lemon juice. Peel the pickling onions but leave whole.

3
Put the mushrooms in a pan with 30 g/1 oz of the butter and 100 ml/3 1/2 fl oz of the veal cooking liquid. Cook for 10 minutes. Put the pickling onions in another pan with 30 g/1 oz of the butter and 200 ml/7 fl oz. Cook until the liquid is absorbed but the onions are still slightly crunchy, about 15 minutes.

4
Remove the veal pieces from the cooking liquid and place in another large pot with the mushrooms and onions. Strain off the vegetables, then return the broth to the same pot and reduce to about 200 ml/7 fl oz. Stir in the remaining butter. Season with a few twists of the peppermill and a generous pinch of nutmeg.

5
Pour the reduced cooking liquid over the meat. In a bowl, whisk together the egg yolks and cream and pour over the meat. Reheat without boiling. Salt if necessary and pepper lightly. Serve.

CHEF'S ADVICE
Blanquette is a traditional French stew for white meat with a characteristic white sauce. This recipe can be prepared up to Step 5, two days in advance and kept in the refrigerator. Just before serving, reheat before adding the cream mixture: must not boil or it will cause the cream and egg to separate.

Quick West Indian Beef Stir Fry

Preparation: 10 minutes
Cooking time: 1-2 minutes
Serves 4

2 long shallots
750 g/1 3/4 lb beef
tenderloin (or sirloin)
1 tablespoon Colombo curry
Seasoning
1/2 bunch chives
2 tablespoons sunflower
or peanut oil
30 g /1 oz unsalted butter
Salt

1
Peel and finely chop the shallots. Cut the meat into
2 cm/1/4 in cubes.

2
Mix together the meat, shallots and Colombo curry.
Snip the chives to obtain 2 tablespoons and set aside.

3
Heat together the oil and butter in a large pan.
Add the meat and cook quickly over high heat
for 1-2 minutes (depending on desired doneness).
Stir in the chives and serve.

CHEF'S ADVICE
*The key to this dish is fast cooking. The meat should be seared
quickly to preserve all the aroma of the spices.*

Spice notes
**Colombo is the West Indian
name for curry powder. Although
it has roots in Asian cuisine,
the flavour of this spice mixture
is completely different! With
a floral, spicy, playful flavour,
use this curry powder to add
punch to an ordinary poached
chicken, stir-fried lamb or
any kind of kebabs.**

overleaf
saffron, four spice blend

Roast Pork
with Indonesian Pepper

**Preparation: 15-20 minutes
(plus marinating overnight)
Cooking time: 1 1/2 hours
Serves 4**

1 pork shoulder, about
1.4 kg/3 lb without the rind
10 long peppers
(Indonesian peppercorns)
Salt
1/2 teaspoon ground cumin
1 teaspoon ground ginger
2 onions
2 tablespoons sunflower
or peanut oil
50 ml/ 1 3/4 fl oz aged
wine vinegar
1 tablespoon soy sauce
1 tablespoon acacia honey
Whole Black pepper
in a peppermill

Spice notes
**The flavour of the Indonesian
pepper will mellow from the long,
slow cooking, thus releasing its
incomparable aroma of exotic,
tropical flowers. Spicy and
lingering, it blends exquisitely
with the tender texture of the meat
and the spiced honey glaze.**

1
One day in advance, make small incisions all over
the meat and fill with the Indonesian peppercorns. In
a small bowl, mix together 1 teaspoon salt, the cumin
and the ginger. Rub the spices all over the meat. Cover
with plastic wrap and refrigerate overnight.

2
The day of serving, preheat the oven to 150° C/300° F.
Peel and coarsely chop the onions. In a large casserole,
heat some oil and add the meat to brown evenly on all
sides. After 5 minutes, add the onion. Cover and bake
for 1 1/4 hour, turning occasionally.

3
Remove the meat from the oven and raise the heat to
210° C/410° F.

4
In a bowl, mix together the vinegar, soy sauce
and honey. Add 6 grinds of the peppermill. Baste
the roast with this sauce and return to the oven for
10 minutes to caramelise. Remove from the oven and
let stand for 10 minutes. Strain the cooking juices.
Slice the pork and serve with the roasting juices.

CHEF'S ADVICE
*For a festive occasion, garnish with deep-fried fresh sage leaves
before serving. A joint with the bone in will taste better.*

Poached Foie Gras

with Vegetables and Tellichery Pepper

Preparation: 30 minutes
Cooking time: 1 3/4 hours
Serves 4

1 whole fresh foie gras, about
500 g/18 oz
1 bunch of turnips with tops
1 bunch of carrots with tops
2 garlic cloves
4 leeks
1 Savoy cabbage
1 1/2 liters/2 1/2 pints
chicken stock (or water)
1 bouquet garni (1 bay leaf
and 2 thyme branches)
Black Tellichery pepper,
whole and ground
200 g/7 oz sugar snap peas
1 small bunch chervil
1 small truffle,
about 15 g/1/2 oz (optional)
1 clove
Brittany sea salt
(or fleur de sel)

Spice notes
**The Tellichery pepper and foie
gras are in complete harmony.
The spice brings out the sweetness
of this delicate ingredient, and
adds a woody and fiery sensation.**

1
To prepare the foie gras, see page 44.

2
Peel the carrots and turnips, leaving a bit of green
at the top of each. Peel the garlic. Clean the leeks
and trim, saving one green bit to wrap around
the bouquet garni, fastened with kitchen string.
Core and quarter the cabbage. Blanch for 5 minutes
in boiling salted water, then drain.

3
Bring the stock (or water) to the boil. Season with the
bouquet garni, 1/2 teaspoon Tellichery peppercorns
and the clove. Cook for 15 minutes, then add
the turnips, carrots, leeks, garlic and cabbage.

4
Preheat the oven to 120° C/250° F. Brown the foie
gras lightly on both sides in a teflon pan, 1-2 minutes.
Pat dry and season with salt and ground Tellichery
pepper. Place in a large pot. Arrange the vegetables
around the foie gras and discard the bouquet garni.
Pour over the stock and bake for 30 minutes.

5
Trim the sugar snap peas and cook for 4 minutes
in boiling salted water. Add them to the foie gras
5 minutes before the end of its cooking time.

6
To serve, slice the foie gras and arrange on a deep
platter with the vegetables and some of the stock.
Grate over the truffle if using and decorate with
whole chervil leaves. Finish with a light sprinkling
of sea salt and ground Tellichery pepper and serve.

CHEF'S ADVICE
*The flavour of this dish, called pot-au-feu in French, comes from
the combination of vegetables. You can vary the selection by season:
in winter replace the sugar snap peas with broccoli, turnips with
parsnips. In spring, use asparagus.*

Duck Breast
with Orange and Cardamom

Preparation: 20 minutes
Cooking time: 25 minutes
Serves 4

2 small onions
3 garlic cloves
I piece fresh ginger
3 tablespoons olive oil
I tablespoon honey
I teaspoon cardamom pods
I tablespoon ketchup
250 ml/9 fl oz fresh orange
juice (about 3 oranges)
I pinch Cayenne pepper
Salt
2 boneless duck breasts,
about 400 g/14 oz each
2 oranges

Spice notes
**The resinous, citrus flavour
of the cardamom is in perfect
harmony with the orange essence.
The sweet-sour note of the sauce
is lightly reinforced by the floral
notes of ginger and Cayenne,
rounding off the symphony
of flavours. The sauce is also
ideal for brushing on pork
spareribs before cooking or,
for something very unusual,
try it with a rack of wild boar
or roast venison haunch.**

I
Peel and chop the onions and garlic. Peel and grate
the ginger to obtain about I tablespoon. Brown lightly
in a pan with some olive oil for 5 minutes.

2
Remove the cardamom seeds from the outer pods and
crush the seeds. Add to the onion mixture, along with
the honey, ketchup, orange juice, Cayenne pepper and
a pinch of salt. Bring to the boil, then remove from the
heat and let stand to infuse while the duck cooks.

3
Make criss-cross incisions in the duck skin. Cook
in a teflon pan, skin-side down, without adding any
oil, for 7 minutes. Discard the cooking fat, turn the
duck, sprinkle with salt and cook on the other side
for 4 minutes.

4
Zest part of an orange, then slice off the pith and
peel from both oranges. Slice the oranges into
rounds. Lightly cook the orange slices in olive oil
for 2 minutes.

5
Remove the duck from the heat, cover and let stand
for 10 minutes. Deglaze the pan with 100 ml/3 1/2 fl oz
water, then add the orange juice mixture. Bring
to the boil and cook for 10 minutes. Strain the sauce
and set aside.

6
Slice the duck breasts widthways and serve with the
cooked orange slices and the sauce. Decorate with
the reserved orange zest.

CHEF'S ADVICE
*The orange-cardamom sauce can be made in advance. When
straining, be sure to press down with a wooden spoon to extract
a maximum of flavour.*

Beef Kebabs with Paprika

**Preparation: 15 minutes
(plus overnight marinating)
Cooking time: 3-5 minutes
Serves 4**

I tablespoon paprika
50 ml/I 3/4 fl oz grapeseed oil
800 g/I 3/4 lb beef cut
in pieces
I fresh thyme sprig
Brittany sea salt
(or fleur de sel)
2 yellow peppers
4 rashers smoked bacon, about
I/2 cm/I/4 in thick each

Spice notes
**The combination of paprika
and beef is reminiscent of
a classic Hungarian goulash,
with its slightly caramelised fruity,
floral aroma. This delightful
dish explodes with flavour,
almost like a boiled lemon sweet.
Try this spice with a chicken
casserole, veal escalopes
or rabbit. Just a few pinches
will transform your meal.**

I
One day before serving, mix three-quarters of
the paprika with the grapeseed oil. Toss with the beef
pieces and sprinkle with the thyme leaves. Cover
with plastic wrap and refrigerate overnight.

2
The day of serving, remove the meat from the
refrigerator and let stand at room temperature.

3
Seed and core the peppers and cut into pieces.
Plunge in boiling water for 30 seconds, then drain.
Set aside.

4
Cut the bacon rashers into 3 pieces. Thread the
beef onto skewers, alternating with the bacon and
pepper pieces. Season with salt. Cook the kebabs
for 3-5 minutes (for rare or medium), either
on the barbecue, under the grill or even on the
hob (for the latter, use some marinade to cook
with). Sprinkle with the remaining paprika and
serve immediately.

CHEF'S ADVICE
*Choose a tender flavoursome cut of beef, rumpsteak is ideal. You
can also use red peppers as they are sweet when grilled, but avoid
green peppers which can be bitter.*

chillies

cayenne pepper *A generic term applied to all hot peppers, originally from Guyana now imported also from India, africa and Zimbabwe.*

birdseye chilli *Tiny red, orange and green chillies. Used mainly in Oriental and West Indian dishes.*

RED, GREEN, YELLOW, ORANGE, BLACK, PURPLE, sweet or spicy, there are thousands of chilli varieties. And they are grown all over the world: India, Indonesia, North Africa, Europe, but especially in South America, where the story of the chilli begins.

Chillies had been growing from the forests of Central America to the Andean plains for thousands of years before the Conquistadors discovered them. Christopher Columbus said chilli was "better than our pepper" (pimienta) and called chillies "pimiento". They were brought back to the Old World, where they quickly brought fire to the cuisines of Africa, Asia and India. More than that, chillies changed the way the world cooked. Spain also adopted this spice, hotter than pepper and much less expensive since it could be cultivated on home soil. Eastern Europe preferred the milder varieties and paprika soon found its way into many dishes, most notably the goulash of Hungary.

cayenne pepper

Ground cayenne is used to flavour many dishes.

espelette peppers

*Conical red shape, dried. This
pepper has an AOC, like fine wine,
and can only be grown in ten
vil'ages surrounding the town of
Espelette in the Basque region
of southwestern France. Excellent
with all fish and shellfish.*

chili con carne seasoning *Paprika, chilli, clove, black pepper, cumin, turmeric.*

Harissa *Crushed garlic and chillies.*

hungarian paprika *Deep red colour, caramelised taste. Use for kebabs and beef stews (goulash).*

house blends

hot pepper blend *A blend of many dried groand chillies chosen to combine flavour and fire. Coconut milk is a good foil for its fiery spice.*

cross-section of a chilli *The seeds have more capsaicin than the flesh.*

The hotness of a chilli comes from capsaicin, which is resistant to the heat of cooking. It is measured in Scoville units, on a scale of 0 to 10. The mildest varieties are ancho and paprika, with a slightly caramelised flavour. Next comes the Mexican pasilla with a slight taste of liquorice, the spicy and flowery Espelette pepper from southwestern France, and the nutty cascabel from Central America. Moving up the scale to number 8 are small, slender Tabascos and tiny red Cayennes. Scalding, lantern-shaped habaneros top the scale at 10.

Dried, whole or ground, chillies are also a common ingredient in spice blends. Combined with garlic in North African harissa, they enflame the broth for a couscous or tajine. Hot chilli and mild paprika dominate the flavour of "chili con carne".

Fresh Espelette peppers
Threaded on a string to dry.

Caramelised Lamb
with Peppercorns

Preparation: 10 minutes
Cooking time: 2 hours 10 minutes
Serves 4

1 onion
1 whole garlic head
3 tablespoons oil
4 lamb shanks (see *Chef's advice*)
30 g/1 oz unsalted butter
Salt
2 teaspoons Five-Berry
mixture
1 tablespoon freshly
grated ginger
8 long shallots
2 sprigs thyme
5 tablespoons aged
wine vinegar
1/2 bunch parsley, chopped

Spice notes
**In the Five-Berry mixture, white
and black peppercorns offer
the classic, balanced pepper taste.
Coriander adds a vegetal note,
backed up by the woodsy
tones of allspice, the lemony
aroma of green peppercorns
and the heather-scent of red
peppercorns. The fatty texture
of the meat conducts this
orchestra of taste to perfection.
Five-Berry mixture is the ideal
all-round seasoning, ready
for anything. It will uplift an
ordinary steak, a duck breast,
even a young wild boar.**

1
Preheat the oven to 150° C/300° F. Peel and chop
the onion. Cut the garlic head in half through
the middle. In a heavy casserole, heat some oil
and add the lamb pieces, cooking until brown
all over, about 5 minutes.

2
Discard the lamb cooking oil and add the butter
and salt to taste. Crush the peppercorns and add
three-quarters to the lamb, along with the onion,
garlic, ginger and thyme. Stir well and add
100 ml/3 1/2 fl oz water.

3
Cover and bake for 1 1/2 hours. Peel the shallots
and arrange them around them around the lamb.
Add the vinegar and 100 ml/3 1/2 fl oz water.
Return to the oven for 30 minutes. Take out
of the oven and remove only the lamb pieces from
the pot; set aside and keep warm.

4
Cook the shallots over high heat, stirring constantly,
until caramelised and brown, about 5 minutes.
Add the lamb pieces and stir to coat with the juices.
Add the rest of the pepper and sprinkle over the
chopped parsley. Serve.

CHEF'S ADVICE
*The best cut of meat for this dish is the shank end of the hind leg,
which is the bit that is usually excluded from a leg of lamb sold at
the supermarket. It is a very tender, melting cut of meat. If you buy
your meat from a butcher, this cut should be obtainable, unless the
butcher has kept it for himself.*

Chicken with Honey-Spice Sauce

**Preparation: 25 minutes
(plus marinating overnight)
Cooking time: 1 hour 10 minutes
Serves 4-6**

FOR THE CHICKEN
125 g/4 oz acacia honey
200 ml/7 fl oz vinegar
2 kg/4 1/2 lb chicken, jointed
1 onion
2 sticks celery
2 tablespoons sunflower
or peanut oil
200 ml/7 fl oz dry white wine
Salt
3 tomatoes (or 200 g/7 oz
chopped peeled tomatoes)
400 ml/3/4 pint chicken
bouillon or stock
200 ml/7 fl oz cream

FOR THE SPICES
2 teaspoons ground
cinnamon
2 teaspoons ground ginger
1 teaspoon cumin seeds
1 container saffron

Spice notes
**Cumin, cinnamon, ginger
and saffron add a perfume
of scented, exotic wood, while
a scent of the North Indian
cuisine comes from citrus,
anise and floral aromas.
The heady, candied aromas
may tempt you to exotic travels;
in the meantime, try this spice
mix with lamb or even vegetable
stew (of courgettes, peppers
and aubergines).**

1
One day before serving, combine all the spices and
set half aside. Blend the other half with the honey
and vinegar. Coat the chicken joints with the honey
mixture, cover with plastic wrap and refrigerate
overnight.

2
The day of serving, peel and chop the onion.
Wash the celery and cut into small pieces. Remove
the chicken from the marinade and drain; reserve
the marinade. In a casserole, brown the chicken in
oil over high heat, about 5 minutes. Watch carefully
as the honey risks caramelising. Remove the chicken,
season with salt and set aside.

3
Add the onion and celery to the pot and cook
for 2 minutes. Add the wine, bring to the boil
and let cook until reduced by half, about 5 minutes.
Add the reserved marinade. Seed and peel the
tomatoes and add.

4
Return the chicken to the pot and add bouillon
or stock to cover. Simmer gently for 40 minutes.
Stir in the cream and the reserved spices.
Cook, uncovered, for 15 minutes so the flavours
intensify. Serve.

CHEF'S ADVICE
*Using a whole chicken adds more flavour to this recipe but you can
also prepare it with individual chicken pieces, such as thighs. If using
breast meat, reduce the cooking time by half. This dish is very
attractive and can be served for festive occasions, decorated with
whole cinnamon sticks and physalis (Cape gooseberries).*

Guinea Fowl Parcels
with Sweet Banyuls Wine, Olives & Black Pepper

Preparation: 30 minutes
Cooking time: 50 minutes
Serves 4

1 free range guinea fowl
about 1.4 kg/3 lb
12 garlic cloves
4 tomatoes
2 onions
8 thin bacon rashers
Olive oil
150 ml/5 1/2 fl oz
Banyuls wine
1 bouquet garni (thyme, bay)
150-200 ml/5 1/2-7 fl oz
bouillon (or water)
125 g/1/4 lb mixed green and
black olives, preferably French
1 lemon
Ground black pepper
Salt

Spice notes
**The pepper flavour is very
predominant here, adding
a herbal taste which will
be enhanced if the guinea fowl
is free range.**

I
Ask your butcher to joint and bone the guinea fowl to
obtain 8 pieces (breasts, thighs and legs).

2
Peel the garlic, cut the cloves in half and remove the
green shoot if any. Cook the garlic pieces in boiling
water for 1 minute to soften. Keep the water and use
to plunge the tomatoes before peeling and seeding
them. Preheat the oven to 180° C/350° F.

3
Peel and chop the onions. Season the guinea fowl
pieces liberally with pepper, then wrap each piece in
bacon and tie with kitchen string. Heat 5 tablespoons
oil in a heavy casserole, add the guinea fowl parcels
and cook to brown, about 3 minutes. Add the onions
and the garlic, crushing it in the pot.

4
Cook the guinea fowl for 2 minutes, then remove
from the pot. Add the Banyuls wine, tomato and
bouquet garni. Cook over high heat for 3 minutes.
Return the guinea fowl to the pot and add the
bouillon.

5
Add the olives. Put the pot in the oven and bake for
30 minutes. Cut the lemon in slices and add, then
continue cooking for a further 10 minutes. Remove
the bouquet garni, taste for seasoning and serve.

CHEF'S ADVICE
*If the olives are very salty, blanch in boiling water for 3 minutes
before adding. Since the bacon is also salty be sure to taste before
seasoning at the end.*

vegetables

& seasonings

Potato Gratin
with Leeks and Spices

Preparation: 30 minutes
Cooking time: 45 minutes
Serves 4

FOR THE GRATIN
2 leeks
40 g/1 1/2 oz unsalted butter
8 waxy potatoes
200 ml/7 fl oz cream
Olive oil
White pepper
Salt

FOR THE SPICES
1 teaspoon cardamom
1 teaspoon cloves
1 teaspoon anise
1 teaspoon Szechuan pepper
Nutmeg

Spice notes
**Szechuan pepper lends a musty
aroma, reinforced by the clove
and resinous scent of cardamom.
Anise is the perfect partner
for leeks. The combination lifts
this gratin out of the ordinary.
Store any remaining spice mix
in an airtight container and
use to season vegetables,
chicken breasts or roast veal.**

1
Prepare the spices: Put all the spices in a spice mill
and grind to a powder. Add a generous grating
of nutmeg. Set aside.

2
Prepare the gratin: Wash the leeks. Trim, leaving
a bit of green for the end. Finely slice the white part.
Cook the leeks in 20 g/3/4 oz butter just to soften,
about 10 minutes. Season to taste with salt and
pepper. Preheat the oven to 150° C/300° F.

3
Peel the potatoes and slice thinly. Season with salt
and 1 teaspoon of the spice mix. Butter the insides
of 4 individual gratin dishes. Dust each with a few
pinches of the spice mix.

4
Put a layer of potatoes in the bottom of each dish.
Pour over some cream, then add a layer of leeks.
Continue layering until all the ingredients are used
up. Finish with the cream.

5
Put the gratin dishes in a hot water bath and bake
for 30 minutes. Meanwhile, thinly slice the reserved
leek greens and stir fry in hot olive oil for 3 minutes.
Remove the gratins from the oven and turn out onto
serving plates. Drain the leek greens and use to
decorate the gratins, with a sprinkling of spice mix
over each.

CHEF'S ADVICE
*To test for doneness, gently insert the tip of a knife into the gratin.
If there is any resistance, continue cooking a bit longer.*

Melting Fennel
with Coriander and Mild Curry

Preparation: 10 minutes
Cooking time: 5 minutes
Serves 4

1/2 lemon
I small bunch fresh coriander
I sweet onion
4 fennel bulbs
White pepper
Salt
I teaspoon mild curry powder
Olive oil

I
Squeeze the lemon juice. Snip the coriander leaves with scissors. Peel the onion and remove the outer fennel leaves; slice both thinly. Bring I litre/I 3/4 pints water to the boil. Add the vegetables. Cook until the water returns to the boil, then remove the fennel and onion. Push down with the back of a large spoon to extract excess liquid.

2
Season the vegetables with salt, pepper and curry. Heat 3 tablespoons oil in a pan, add the vegetables and cook over high heat for 2–3 minutes, stirring constantly. Add the lemon juice and coriander. Serve immediately.

Spice notes
The brief, stir-fry method of cooking intensifies the caramelised, floral aromas from the turmeric in the curry powder. It also enhances the spicy, dried fruit flavour of the mustard. Anise and cumin add spice and bring out the vegetal tastes of the fennel. This is delicious when served with Mediterranean fish, such as red mullet, gurnard, or whole grilled sea bass.

CHEF'S ADVICE
This dish owes its delicacy to the way in which the fennel is sliced. It must be very thin, almost transparent, as if it had been sliced by machine.

Mini Peppers
with Green Peppercorn Stuffing

Preparation: 30 minutes
Cooking time: 45 minutes
Serves 4

Whole freeze-dried green
peppercorns
100 g/3 1/2 oz fresh spinach
1/2 carrot
1 small onion
200 g/7 oz sausage meat
1 boneless duck breast, about
200 g/7 oz
A handful of fresh bread-
crumbs
1 egg
50 ml/ 1 3/4 fl oz milk
1 small bunch parsley
Brittany sea salt
(or fleur de sel)
Four Spice blend
16 mini peppers
200 ml/7 fl oz bouillon
Olive oil

1
Put 1 teaspoon green peppercorns in water to
rehydrate. Meanwhile, wash and trim the spinach.
Cook in boiling water for 30 seconds, then drain.

2
Peel and chop the carrot and onion. Heat 1 tablespoon oil in a pan, add the carrot and onion and
cook gently to soften, about 10 minutes. Finely chop
the spinach. Preheat the oven to 180° C/350° F.

3
Remove the skin from the duck, then cut into
small cubes. Put in a bowl with the spinach. Add
the sausage meat, carrot, onion, breadcrumbs, egg,
milk, chopped parsley and salt. Season with a
knifepoint of Four Spice blend and the drained
green peppercorns.

4
Slice the top bit off the mini peppers and gently tap
out any seeds. Fill the peppers with the sausage
mixture and replace the pepper tops like lids. Put
in a dish with the bouillon and bake for 35 minutes,
basting occasionally with the bouillon. Serve.

Spice notes
**Clove, nutmeg, white pepper
and cinnamon make up the Four
Spice blend and they are the
traditional seasoning for sausages,
potted meat and other charcuterie
items. They lend a pronounced
bark flavour, while the green
pepper adds spice and herbal
tones. The combination adds
a tremendous floral bouquet
to the stuffing. Use this recipe
to stuff other vegetables: tomatoes,
courgette blossoms, red onions
or aubergines. It is also
delicious as a stuffing for oily
fish, especially sardines.**

CHEF'S ADVICE
*Serve with roast meat or poultry (lamb, chicken, rabbit), or with
fish. This can also be served cold, as a nibble with aperitifs.*

Aubergine Compote
with Star Anise

**Preparation: 25 minutes
(plus overnight marinating)
Cooking time: 35 minutes
Serves 4**

1 thyme sprig
1 small celery stick with leaves
1 lemon
Salt
1 teaspoon cloves
3 star anise
1 teaspoon fennel seeds
4 aubergines
Olive oil

Spice notes
Cooking aubergine in this manner, with spices from all over the world, gives it an Eastern taste. Clove reminds of India and star anise lends a taste of the Orient. Try this spice when poaching or marinating shellfish.

1
Tie the thyme and celery together with kitchen string to make a bouquet garni. Bring 50 ml/1 3/4 fl oz water to the boil with the juice of the lemon, a generous pinch of salt, the bouquet garni and the spices. Lower the heat and simmer gently for 15 minutes.

2
Peel the aubergines and slice into rounds, then cut into cubes. Cook the aubergine cubes in the spiced water and return to the boil. Add more salt and cook for 10 minutes. Remove the aubergine cubes with a slotted spoon and set aside.

3
Continue cooking the spiced water until reduced by three-quarters, about 10 minutes. Pour over the aubergine and let cool. Drizzle with olive oil to cover. Refrigerate until needed.

CHEF'S ADVICE
Advance preparation allows time for the flavours to mingle and will greatly enhance this dish. It can be prepared as much as 2 days in advance but be sure to keep the aubergine covered with oil until needed. Serve as an accompaniment to fish or with cold meats, such as leftover pork or lamb roast.

Basmati Rice with Indian Spices

Preparation: 15 minutes
Cooking time: 20 minutes
Serves 4

I piece fresh ginger
I onion
I tablespoon blanched almonds
300 g/11 oz basmati rice
Oil
Pepper
Salt
I teaspoon cinnamon
2 star anise
3 cardamom pods
I teaspoon anise
I tablespoon shelled pistachios
I container ground saffron
30 g/1 oz unsalted butter

Spice notes
**Split open the cardamom pods
to release the full aroma of
the black seeds. The rice is very
absorbent and becomes saturated
with the perfume of anise
and cardamom. This is a highly
aromatic dish with all the heady
scents of Indian cuisine. Serve
with roast chicken or lamb,
or baked fish.**

1
Peel and grate the ginger to obtain 1 tablespoon.
Peel and finely chop the onion. Cut the almonds
into 2-3 pieces. Preheat the oven to 240° C/475° F.
Bring 1 litre/1 3/4 pints water to the boil.

2
Rinse the rice under running water. In a heavy
casserole, cook the onion in 2 tablespoons oil until
soft. After 5 minutes, add the drained rice, ginger
and salt and pepper to taste. Stir for 2 minutes.

3
Add all the spices, except the saffron, and stir. Add
water to cover the rice by about 2 cm/1 in. Bring to
the boil and add the almonds and pistachios. Cover
and cook in the oven for 10 minutes.

4
Dissolve the saffron in a bit of water. Remove
the rice from the oven, add the bits of butter and the
saffron. Let stand, without stirring, for 5 minutes
before serving.

CHEF'S ADVICE
*You can also cook the rice by covering and leaving over low heat
until the liquid is completely absorbed.*

overleaf
star anise, coriander seeds

Bulghur Wheat
with Dried Fruit and Ras-El-Hanout

Preparation: 2 hours
(plus 2 hours refrigeration)
No cooking time
Serves 4

200 g/7 oz bulghur wheat
70 g/2 1/2 oz soft dried
apricots
2 tablespoons pine nuts
1/2 bunch fresh coriander
1/2 bunch fresh parsley
1 teaspoon Ras-El-Hanout
Spice blend
1 pinch cumin
Olive oil
Ground white pepper
Salt

1
Rinse the bulghur in a colander under running water until the water runs clear and all the starch has been eliminated. Drain well and transfer to a large bowl. Add water to cover and let stand for 1 1/2 hours. The grains should not be completely soft.

2
Dice the apricots. Toast the pine nuts in a dry teflon pan and set aside. Strip the leaves from the coriander and parsley stems and chop finely.

3
Drain the bulghur and toss with your hands to remove as much moisture as possible. Stir in the herbs, apricots, pine nuts and spices. Season with salt and a generous pinch of white pepper. Drizzle generously with olive oil (about 100 ml/3 1/2 fl oz). Refrigerate for 2 hours before serving.

Spice notes
Ras-el-hanout is a North African spice mixture that combines the heady scents of coriander, turmeric, cumin, caraway and chilli. The taste is a combination of chilli spice and full-bodied anise, and is the perfect complement to dishes with dried fruit and fresh herbs. Try using some in a marinade for lamb or chicken.

CHEF'S ADVICE
The wheat will absorb even more flavour if the dish is made one day in advance. In this case, do not add the herbs until ready to serve. This is the perfect dish for a summer buffet and is delicious with honey-roasted chicken.

Tomato and Fennel Compote
with Lemongrass

Preparation: 25 minutes
Cooking time: 40 minutes
Serves 4

1 kg/2 lb 3 oz ripe tomatoes
1 fennel bulb
6 spring onions
2 garlic cloves
1 tablespoon pine nuts
1 pinch Cayenne pepper
1 pinch turmeric
1 pinch cumin
1 pinch ginger
1 sprig thyme
3 stalks dried lemongrass
Olive oil
Salt

Spice notes
This spice mix is very similar to curry. It adds a smooth, mellow quality to the tomatoes, reinforced by the onions. Lemongrass and fennel, a bit of anise and citrus, add contrast with their lively sensation of freshness. Serve this thick sauce with any kind of pasta: fusilli, penne, etc. It is equally delicious with grilled fish.

1
Peel, seed and chop the tomatoes. Remove the outer leaves from the fennel bulb and cut into small cubes. Peel and chop the onions. Peel and crush the garlic. Toast the pine nuts in a dry teflon pan.

2
Heat 50 ml/1 3/4 fl oz oil in a pot. Add the onions, fennel and garlic and cook over low heat for 10 minutes. Add the tomatoes, spices, thyme and lemongrass. Season to taste.

3
Cover and lower the heat. Cook for 30 minutes, adding the pine nuts halfway through. Remove the thyme and lemongrass. Serve.

CHEF'S ADVICE
You can also add basil, capers and parmesan.
In summer, when ripe tomatoes are plentiful, make extra and refrigerate, or freeze. In winter, this can be made with chopped peeled tomatoes in tins.

woody spices

turmeric rhizome *Dried and crushed, it can be used for shellfish, fish and rice.*

cardamom pods *The spice is inside the pods, in two rows of seeds. The largest pods can contain as many as twenty. Use to flavour sweet or savoury marinades, tea or jams.*

WITH THEIR AROMA OF PINE FOREST, myrtle, camphor, turpentine and resin, these spices evoke the image of ancient caravans crossing the desert. Nutmeg comes from a large evergreen green tree with highly scented leaves which bears an apricot-sized fruit. After ripening, the fruit splits open to reveal an inner stone surrounded by a lacy yellow membrane. The membrane, known as mace, takes two weeks to dry, the stone, or nutmeg, requires two months, making it easy to break the mace to release the nutmeg. The tree is native to the Moluccas, or Spice Islands and for a long time, cultivation was the monopoly of the Dutch. Eventually, the French exported trees to the Mauritian Islands, then to Indonesia, Malaysia, and especially Grenada in the West Indies.

Clove, often called the "honey of the spice route", was greatly appreciated by Mandarin Chinese who chewed it as a breath freshener. Also the fruit of a tree with the same origin as nutmeg, cloves are now grown in Madagascar, Malaysia, Zanzibar and Pemba (an island in the Indian Ocean). The flower

cloves *These contain eugenol, which is antiseptic and aids the digestion. Use in stews and marinades. Clove-studded oranges can be used to scent wardrobes.*

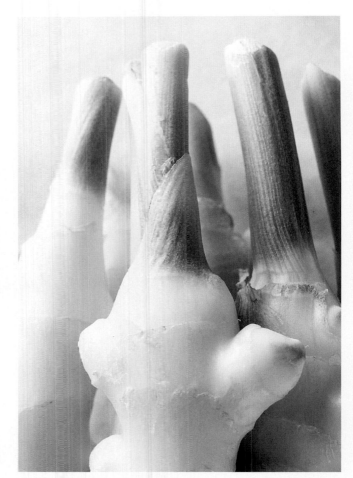

young ginger *Becomes more gnarled as it grows. Ground ginger can be used on shellfish, chicken, pork spareribs, tarts and cakes.*

yellow mustard *Tiny golden seeds which are spicy and slightly nutty-sweet. Use to flavour vinegar. Sprouted seeds can be sprinkled over salads.*

allspice *Not a peppercorn, the wrinkled skin has the strongest aroma. Use in marinades for game, red meat or for stewed fruit.*

juniper *Only dried berries are used. Their pine flavour is best for marinating game and sauer kraut.*

mace *Dried aril (the outer case) of nutmeg with a subtle orange peel aroma. Use for marinades and stewed fruit.*

colombo *Turmeric, cumin, caraway.*

four spice blend *White pepper, clove, nutmeg, cinnamon.*

hot curry *Clove, turmeric, mustard, coriander, cumin, chilli, anise, fenugreek, fennel, garlic, salt. Medium and mild curry powders have less chilli.*

house blends

nutmeg *Grate over potato gratins and vegetables. Ground nutmeg is good for quiches.*

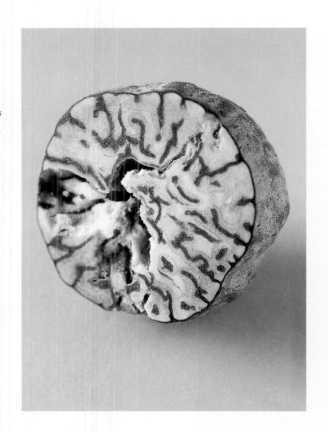

buds go from green to yellow and then to pink, when they are harvested, just before full maturation. The buds are pulled from the stems and dried. Ground cloves lend a resinous aroma to spice blends and with their strong, cooling flavour, they soften the fire of curry blends.

Allspice has a flavour that combines clove, nutmeg and cinnamon, hence the name. It comes from a tree in the myrtle family, grown in the Caribbean. The tree bears fruit with two berries, which look a bit like peas and which darken as they dry. Allspice can be used in sweet and savoury dishes.

Cardamom seeds are hidden inside pods. They have an aroma of camphor, lemon and eucalyptus. They come from a plant which grows on the hillsides of southern India, as well as in Central America. The fruits of this plant are harvested manually and left to dry in the sun. Cardamom is said to have aphrodisiac qualities; it certainly adds zing to Arabic coffee and a luscious scent to garam masala mixtures as well as many Indian desserts.

Ginger is a staple of Oriental cuisine; it is pepper, salt and seasoning all rolled into one. It can be sweet when candied, or savoury when pickled in vinegar. Ginger dries well and in its ground form makes a delicious addition to honey-roasted chicken, chocolate desserts or baked rhubarbor apples.

Turmeric comes from the underground rhizome of a plant with large lily-like leaves. It is related to ginger and cardamom. When sliced, turmeric reveals its highly scented yellow flesh with a clear, floral aroma tinged with a hint of bitterness. Turmeric is grown mostly in India. The rhizome is boiled, then dried and ground to a powder and used to colour curries and colombos (West Indian curry). Turmeric is also used to add colour to prepared mustard.

Preserved Lemon
with Five-Berry Mixture

Marinating time: 3 days
Cooking time: 3 x 20 minutes
(once a day over the 3 days)
Makes 2 1L/1 3/4 pints jars

12 small unwaxed,
organic lemons
400 g/14 oz caster sugar
Coarse salt
1 piece fresh ginger
2 birdseye chillies
250 ml/9 fl oz dry white wine
1 tablespoon Five-Berry
Mixture
2 star anise
2 cinnamon sticks
1 teaspoon juniper berries

Spice notes
**The lemon peel becomes
impregnated with all the spices
and is good enough to eat on
its own, a bit like candied ginger.
It is an explosion of flavours,
from the fiery spice of the chilli
to the woody, resinous flavour
of the Five Berry mixture.
The hint of star anise adds
a light, subtle note which is
delicious with fish.**

1
Scrub the lemons under running water, then dry.
Make 2 lengthwise slits from the stem end to the
bottom. Mix together 100 g/3 1/2 oz sugar and
5 tablespoons salt. Stuff this mixture into the sliced
parts of the lemons. Set aside for half a day.

2
Peel the ginger and slice into thin sticks to obtain
1 tablespoon. Remove the seeds from the chillies.
Put 1 litre/1 3/4 pints water in a pot large enough
to hold all the ingredients. Add the wine, the rest
of the sugar, and all the spices and flavourings.
Marinate for 1 hour. Bring to the boil.

3
Rinse the sugar and salt off the lemons. Put in
the spiced wine mixture, which should completely
submerge the lemons. Cover and simmer gently for
20 minutes. Let cool, then refrigerate for 24 hours.

4
Repeat step 3 twice more, but keep using the same
spiced liquid mixture and add water as necessary. After
the third marinating day, divide the lemons between
2 jars and pour over the spiced liquid to cover.

CHEF'S ADVICE
*This is a cheat's recipe for preserved lemons; the traditional method
requires 3–4 weeks standing time. Use the preserved lemon peel
to flavour salads, grilled fish or tajines (stews). To store, keep in
the refrigerator for 3 weeks, ensuring the lemons are covered with
the liquid at all times. To keep longer, drain off the liquid and add
olive oil to cover completely.*

Spiced Olive Oil

Preparation: 15 minutes
(plus 12 hours marinating time)
Cooking time: 5 minutes
Makes 1 litre/1 3/4 pints

1 teaspoon fennel seed
1 teaspoon caraway seeds
10 cardamom pods
10 juniper berries
1 pinch saffron strands
1 litre/1 3/4 pints
fruity olive oil

1
Toast the fennel and caraway seeds in a dry teflon pan for 30 seconds. Remove the black cardamom seeds from their pods.

2
Put all the seeds and spices in a pot. Add the oil.

3
Gently warm the oil over low heat; it should not boil. Remove from the heat. Let stand for 12 hours. Strain and pour into one or several bottles. Store in a cool, dark place.

Spice notes
**With its aromas of fennel
and saffron, just a splash of this
spiced oil will transport you
to the seaside in Southern France.
Juniper and cardamom add
a touch of pine forest.**

CHEF'S ADVICE
The oil with bubble gently at 65° C/150° F. Use this oil to season green salads, raw fish dishes or grilled fish. It can also be used as a marinade for fish.

Vinegar
with Clove and Sarawak Pepper

**Preparation: 10 minutes
(3 weeks marinating time)
Cooking time: 30 seconds
Makes 1 litre/1 3/4 pints**

1 piece fresh ginger
2 shallots (or 1 tablespoon
freeze-dried shallots)
2 cardamom pods
3 cloves
1 star anise
1 teaspoon whole Sarawak
peppercorns
Nutmeg
Peel of 1/2 orange
20 g/3/4 oz Brittany sea salt
(or fleur de sel)
1/4 teaspoon mustard seeds
1 litre/1 3/4 pints
wine vinegar

) *Spice notes*
**The dominant flavours here
are the woody spices (clove and
Sarawak pepper) and the orange
peel. Ginger and cardamom
reinforce and enhance the overall
strength while the mustard both
tones down and adds spice. A few
drops of this vinegar will enliven
a humble pork chop and enhance
duck breast or sautéed foie gras.**

1
Peel the ginger then cut into sticks to obtain
1 tablespoon. Peel the shallot then cut in half.
Remove the cardamom seeds from their pods.

2
Gently crush the spices: clove, cardamom, star anise
and peppercorns. Put them all in a dry teflon pan and
toast for just a few seconds to release the essential oils.

3
Put the toasted spices in a glass or ceramic bowl.
Add a generous grating of nutmeg, the orange peel,
ginger, shallot, mustard seeds, salt and vinegar.
Mix, cover and keep in a cool place for 3 weeks.

4
Strain the vinegar and transfer to one or several small
bottles. Seal and store in a cool, dark place.

CHEF'S ADVICE
*To completely remove all the marinating ingredients, strain the
vinegar through a fine sieve and then through a coffee filter. Use
different kinds of vinegar to vary the results: cider vinegar, sherry
vinegar, aged wine vinegar, etc.*

desserts

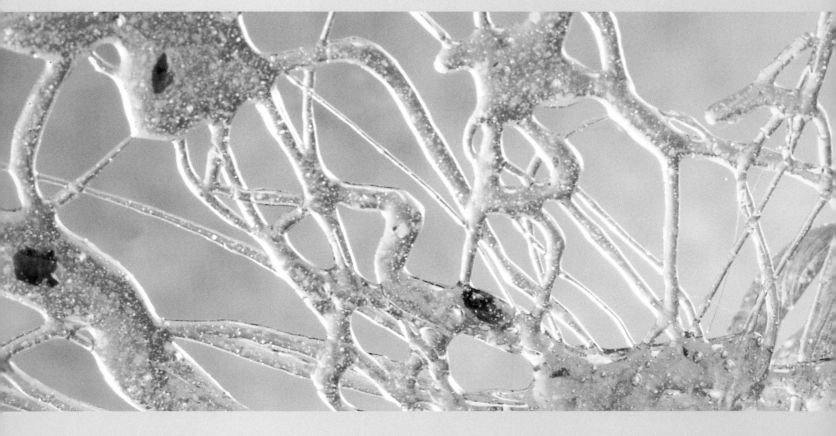

& sweets

Spiced Fruit Compote
with Gingerbread Spice Ice Cream

**Preparation: 40 minutes
(1 day in advance)
Cooking time: 35 minutes
Serves 4**

FOR THE FRUIT
3 comice pears
2 cox apples
1 tablespoon lemon zest,
plus juice of 1 lemon
50 g/1 3/4 oz caster sugar
1 tablespoon orange zest
35 g/1 1/4 oz chestnut honey
35 g/ 1 1/4 oz unsalted butter
65 g/2 1/4 oz dried apricots
65 g/ 2 1/4 oz shelled hazelnuts
1 pinch ground vanilla
2 pinches Pain d'épices seasoning

FOR THE ICE CREAM
400 ml/14 fl oz milk
100 ml double cream
2 tablespoons chestnut honey
100 g/3 1/2 oz sugar
4 pinches Pain d'épices seasoning
1 pinch ground vanilla
5 egg yolks

Spice notes
**The Pain d'épices mixture is
a combination of smooth, mellow
spices, with a predominant note
of cinnamon, heightened by
the sharp freshness of anise and
ginger. The flavours of autumn
fruit – the depth of the cox apples
and the honeyed pear – combine
with the ice cream to distil the
spices. Each mouthful reminds of
sweet-scented nursery puddings.**

1
One day before serving, prepare the ice cream:
Combine the milk, cream and honey in a pan and
bring to the boil. In another pan, heat half the sugar
until it becomes a deep golden caramel. Remove
from the heat and carefully pour in the milk mixture.
Stir in the spices.

2
Whisk the egg yolks with the remaining sugar until
thick and lemon coloured. Slowly pour the milk
mixture onto the eggs, stirring. Return to the heat
and cook, stirring constantly without boiling, until
it is thick enough to coat the back of the spoon.
Let cool, then strain. Freeze in an ice cream maker
according to manufacturer's instructions.

3
Prepare the compote: Peel the fresh fruit and cut into
cubes. Toss with the lemon juice. Add the sugar,
citrus zest and honey.

4
In a heavy casserole, melt the butter until it turns
golden brown. Add three-quarters of the fruit and
stir. Cover and cook for 15 minutes. Add the
remaining fruit and cook, uncovered, for a further
10 minutes.

5
Dice the apricots. Stir into the compote along with
the hazelnuts, vanilla and Pain d'épices spice mix.
Refrigerate overnight.

6
Serve the fruit compote with scoops of the ice cream.

CHEF'S ADVICE
*For a smoother ice cream, add a pinch of agar-agar to the mixture.
The ice cream also makes a delicious dessert served with the Tuile
Biscuits (see page 162).*

Grapefruit Salad
with Raspberry Sorbet & Star Anise Sauce

Preparation: 25 minutes
(plus 3 hours marinating time)
Cooking time: 1 minute
Serves 4

FOR THE GRAPEFRUIT SALAD
2 grapefruits, preferably pink
100 g/3 1/2 oz sliced
gingerbread
300 ml/ 1/2 pint
raspberry sorbet
125 g/4 oz raspberries

FOR THE STAR ANISE SAUCE
50 g/1 3/4 oz caster sugar
1 star anise
1 pinch ground cinnamon
1 teaspoon grated orange peel

Spice notes
**Star anise lends its elegant
and refined flavour. Orange
peel and cinnamon add a touch
of floral bouquet which is carried
over to the sorbet. The fresh
raspberries round out the
recipe, adding a hint of fruity
boiled sweets.**

1
Prepare the sauce: bring 250 ml/9 fl oz water to the
boil. Add the sugar, orange peel, cinnamon and star
anise. Remove from the heat and let stand for 1 hour.

2
Strain and refrigerate for 2 hours.

3
Prepare the salad: Slice off the skin and pith from
each grapefruit. Cut in half, then into quarters.
Refrigerate for 2 hours.

4
Put 4 dessert plates in the freezer for 10 minutes.
Toast the gingerbread slices lightly and cut into sticks
while still warm. Remove the sorbet from the freezer
and let stand at room temperature for 5 minutes
to soften slightly.

5
Drizzle a bit of the star anise sauce on each plate.
Top with slices of grapefruit and scoops of sorbet.
Decorate with fresh raspberries. Serve with
the gingerbread "croutons" and the remaining sauce.

CHEF'S ADVICE
*Raspberry sorbet is quite simple to make at home. Here is an easy
recipe: Warm 100 ml/3 1/2 fl oz water with 1 tablespoon honey.
Add 75 g/2 3/4 oz sugar and 1/2 teaspoon agar-agar. Bring to
the boil. Pour this over 250 g/9 oz fresh raspberry pulp mixed with
the juice of half a lemon. Add 3 pinches cinnamon. Mix and freeze
in a sorbet maker according to instructions.*

Roasted Pineapple
with Indonesian Pepper

**Preparation: 25 minutes
(6 hours marinating time)
Cooking time: 30 minutes
Serves 4**

2 allspice berries
1/4 teaspoon Szechuan
pepper
2 cloves
30 g/1 oz acacia honey
1 vanilla pod,
Bourbon if possible
1 pineapple, about
1.2 kg/2 1/2 lb
6 long peppers
(Indonesian peppercorns)

Spice notes
**Softened by the acidity of the
fruit, the Indonesian pepper
melts in the mouth and leaves
a smouldering floral taste.
It is balanced by the smooth
pepperyness of the Bourbon
vanilla. Allspice and Szechuan
pepper add to the sensual tropical
aromas, which whisk us away on
a journey down the Spice Route.**

1
Combine the allspice, Szechuan pepper and cloves in
a peppermill and grind. Add the spices to the honey.
Cut the vanilla pod into 8 pieces.

2
To peel the pineapple decoratively, use the tip of
a small knife to trace the lines of eyes that twist all
around the pineapple. Cut through the traced lines
slanting the knife at a 45 degree angle, then slice
along the other side of the same line, slanting the
knife in the opposite direction so that the cut meets
in the middle. Alternatively, slice the skin away,
cutting deep enough to remove the eyes.

3
Stud the pineapple with the Indonesian pepper and
vanilla pieces. Pour over the spiced honey. Marinate
in the refrigerator for 6 hours, basting occasionally.

4
Preheat the oven to 200° C/400° F. Cook the
pineapple on a spit. Alternatively set it on a rack
over a roasting dish filled with the marinade
which has been diluted with some water (this will
prevent the honey from caramelising too quickly).
Roast for 30 minutes, basting often. Serve.

CHEF'S ADVICE
*Serve this warm, with vanilla ice cream or custard. This is also an
unusual accompaniment for savoury dishes, such as honey braised
gammon (studded with cloves).*

Coffee Creams with Cardamom

**Preparation: 25 minutes
(plus 3 hours refrigeration)
Cooking time: 5-10 minutes
Serves 4**

2 gelatine sheets
8 candied orange quarters
400 ml/14 fl oz cream
5 egg yolks
100 ml/3 1/2 fl oz espresso
coffee
120 g/4 oz demerara sugar
Ground cardamom

1
Soften the gelatine sheets in a bowl of cold water.
Cut the candied oranges into small cubes. In a bowl,
combine the cream, egg yolks, espresso, diced orange,
sugar and 3 pinches of cardamom.

2
Set the bowl of cream over another bowl of hot water.
Stir until thick enough to coat the back of the spoon.
Squeeze the excess water from the gelatine sheets
and add.

3
Divide the mixture between individual ramekins
(the shallow type). Let cool, then refrigerate 3 hours
before serving.

Spice notes
**Ground cardamom releases
powerful mentholated aroma,
which contrasts beautifully
with the woody, citrusy flavours.
The mingling odours of sweet
coffee and cardamom will
transport you to a faraway North
African souk.**

CHEF'S ADVICE
*For home-made candied oranges, slice 1 orange into 8 sections.
Cook the oranges in boiling water, changing the water three times,
to soften the skin. Make a sugar syrup of 100 g/3 1/2 oz sugar,
200 ml/7 fl oz water and a pinch of cardamom. Add the orange
sections and cook until the oranges are transparent. Let stand in the
syrup overnight before using.*

overleaf
long pepper, cardamom

Chocolate-Ginger Cake

Preparation: 30 minutes
Cooking time: 55 minutes
Serves 4-6

2 unwaxed organic oranges
4 eggs
200 g/7 oz sugar
40 g/ 1 1/2 oz best dark
chocolate (77%)
70 g/2 1/2 oz unsalted butter
4 tablespoons crème fraîche
2 pinches salt
220 g/8 oz flour
2 teaspoons baking powder
40 g/1 1/2 oz unsweetened
cocoa powder
2-3 teaspoons ground ginger
2 tablespoons kirsch

Spice notes
**Orange peel enhances the flavour
of the chocolate. The highly
perfumed ground ginger adds
a lingering freshness, and serves
as a link between the pepper
and floral aromas. This is
a classic afternoon tea cake.**

1
Preheat the oven to 180° C/350° F. Grate the orange
peel. Break the eggs into a bowl. Add the sugar
and orange peel and beat well.

2
Break the chocolate into pieces and put in a bowl.
Add the butter. Melt over a water bath (or in a
microwave) without stirring. Warm the crème fraîche
and add, with the salt. Fold in the egg mixture.

3
In a large bowl, sift together the flour, baking
powder, cocoa and ginger. Fold into the chocolate
mixture in batches. Add the kirsch.

4
Pour the batter into a 26 cm/10 in teflon cake tin
(or grease an ordinary tin). Bake for 45 minutes.
Test for doneness by inserting the tip of a knife
in the middle of the cake. It is done when the blade
comes out clean. Continue baking 5-10 minutes
if necessary.

5
Turn out onto a cooling rack while still warm. Serve
with an orange fruit salad or bitter orange marmalade.

CHEF'S ADVICE
*If not using a teflon tin, line with baking parchment as well to make
the cake easier to turn out.*

Custard Cream with Tonka Beans

Preparation: 30 minutes
Cooking time: 45 minutes
Serves 4

1 tonka bean
200 g/ 7 oz sugar
450 ml/3/4 pint milk
1/2 vanilla pod
1/2 orange
2 eggs
2 egg yolks

Spice notes
Tonka beans come from the Coumarou tree. In this recipe, they take on a caramelised, almost chocolate taste, with just a hint of anise. Combined with custard, they leave a pleasant lingering sensation which enhances the smoothness of the vanilla. Tonka beans should not be used in large quantities or the taste will become overbearing and unpleasant, with an almost artificial flavour.

1
Line a baking sheet with parchment paper. Grind the tonka bean in a spice mill. Put 125 g/4 oz sugar in a pan and heat until it becomes a golden caramel. Remove from the heat and carefully stir in half the tonka bean. Spread on the prepared baking sheet and let cool.

2
Preheat the oven to 180° C/350° F. Bring the milk to the boil with the rest of the sugar. Split the vanilla pod and scrape out the black seeds into the milk. Add the grated orange peel and the rest of the tonka bean. Let stand for 10 minutes.

3
Beat the eggs and pour in the warm milk. Strain. Break the cooled caramel into pieces and reserve 4 for the decoration. Divide the caramel pieces between 4 10 cm/4 in ramekins. Pour over the custard mixture.

4
Put the ramekins in a water bath, cover with aluminium and bake for 35 minutes. Let cool, then refrigerate. To serve, turn out and decorate with the reserved caramel pieces. Serve on its own, or with the Cherry Compote (see page 167).

CHEF'S ADVICE
If your ramekins are smaller than 10 cm/4 in, simply use a few more. Any leftovers can be kept for 2–3 days in the refrigerator.

Spiced Almond Tart
with Fresh Fruit

Preparation: 40 minutes
(1 1/2 hours in advance
for the pastry)
Cooking time: 30 minutes
Serves 4-6

FOR THE SWEET PASTRY
120 g/4 oz unsalted butter,
softened, plus extra for the tin
75 g/2 3/4 oz icing sugar
25 g/1 oz ground almonds
2 pinches fine Brittany sea salt
(or fleur de sel)
2 pinches powdered vanilla
1 egg
200 g/7 oz flour

FOR THE FILLING
2 pinches powdered
Bourbon vanilla
2 pinches ground cinnamon
1 pinch ground ginger
70 g/ 2 1/2 oz icing sugar
70 g/2 1/2 oz unsalted butter
1 egg
80 g/2 3/4 oz ground almonds
1 tablespoon cornstarch
1 tablespoon kirsch
100 ml/3 1/2 fl oz double cream

FOR THE TOPPING
125 g/4 oz of each fruit:
raspberries, redcurrants,
blackcurrants
4 apricots

1
Prepare the pastry: Combine the butter, icing sugar, ground almonds, salt, vanilla, egg and flour. Mix just enough to blend and form into a ball; do not overmix. Refrigerate for 1 1/2 hours.

2
Preheat the oven to 180° C/350° F. Grease a 23 cm/9 in tart tin. Roll out half the dough and line the tin. Cover with baking parchment and fill with baking weights (or dried beans). Bake for 15 minutes. Remove the paper and weights and let cool; keep the oven on.

3
Make the filling: combine the spices and icing sugar. Using an electric mixer, beat the butter and spiced sugar together. Add the egg, ground almonds, cornstarch and kirsch. Lightly whip the cream and mix in.

4
Pour the filling into the tart case. Bake for 12-15 minutes. Let cool. Decorate with apricot slices and the berries.

CHEF'S ADVICE
The pastry is easier to handle if made in large batches which is why this quantity is more than you will need, but it freezes very well. This tart can be made year-round with whatever fruit is in season: peaches, figs or plums, and in winter use peeled sliced citrus fruit or grated apple tossed in lemon juice.

) *Spice notes*
The ginger and cinnamon in the filling give a slight gingerbread flavour, but the powerful, heady Bourbon vanilla dominates.

Chocolate Creams
with Sweet Chilli Sauce

Preparation: 45 minutes
Cooking time: 15-20 minutes
Serves 4

FOR THE CREAMS
120 g/4 oz unsalted butter, plus
extra for the tins
6 pinches sweet chilli pepper
(paprika)
160 g/6 oz best dark chocolate
1 egg
3 egg yolks
30 g/1 oz caster sugar

FOR THE CARAMEL SAUCE
55 g/2 oz sugar
2 tablespoons warm milk
100 ml/3 1/2 fl oz double cream
25 g/1 oz best dark chocolate,
broken in pieces
1 teaspoon unsalted butter

FOR THE CHILLI SAUCE
35 g/1 1/4 oz sugar
1 teaspoon cornstarch
2-3 pinches sweet chilli pepper

Spice notes
**The sweet chilli, or paprika,
explodes in a burst of warm
caramelised fruit. It is further
enhanced by the buttery, milky
aromas, which add to the intensity
of the chocolate. This is inspired
by the Inca tradition of serving
hot chocolate seasoned with hot
chilli. This can also be made with
long pepper (Indonesian pepper),
which has a scent of tropical
flowers that goes nicely with
the chocolate.**

1
Prepare the caramel sauce: Heat the sugar in a pan
until it turns a deep caramel colour. Remove from
the heat and carefully add the milk, then the cream.
Bring to the boil. Put the chocolate pieces in a bowl
and pour over one-third of the hot caramel milk.
Stir then repeat twice until completely blended.
Let cool slightly then whisk in the butter. Refrigerate
until needed.

2
Prepare the creams: Melt the butter over low heat.
Add the chilli and let stand 20 minutes. Break
the chocolate into pieces and melt in a water bath.
With an electric mixer, beat the egg, egg yolks and
sugar. Add the melted chocolate and butter. Grease
4 7 cm/3 in ramekins and pour in the mixture.
Preheat the oven to 200° C/400° F.

3
Prepare the chilli sauce: Heat 20 g/3/4 oz sugar
until it caramelises. Carefully add 150 ml/5 1/2 fl oz
water and the cornstarch. Bring to the boil, then
add the rest of the sugar and the chilli. Let stand
for 20 minutes.

4
Meanwhile, put the creams in the oven and bake for
8 minutes. Let stand for 10 minutes. To serve, drizzle
the caramel and chilli sauces onto 4 plates. Turn out
the creams onto the plates.

CHEF'S ADVICE
*To avoid lumps, dissolve the cornstarch in a bit of water before
adding to the caramel.*

Strawberry Salad
with Mint and Sarawak Pepper

**Preparation: 15 minutes
(plus 2 hours refrigeration)
Cooking time: 1 minutes
Serves 4**

1 lemon
85 g/3 oz caster sugar
1 big bunch fresh peppermint
Whole black Sarawak
peppercorns
650 g/1 1/2 lb strawberries
in season
1 tablespoon olive oil
1 teaspoons demerara
or coarse sugar

Spice notes
**Sarawak pepper takes on the role
of lemon juice in this recipe as
it serves to heighten the flavour
of the berries. The addition
of mint is an explosive one,
giving a blast of peppery, vegetal,
fresh flavours. Olive oil serves as
a gentle background, allowing the
flavours to blend in the mouth.
Sarawak pepper is also good with
peaches, especially white peaches.**

1
Prepare the pepper syrup: Grate half the lemon zest. Put the sugar in a pan with 500 ml/16 fl oz water and bring to the boil. Add the lemon zest, half the mint bundle and 8 grinds of Sarawak pepper. Let infuse in the refrigerator for 1 hour.

2
Wash and trim the strawberries, then cut in half or quarters depending on size. Refrigerate while the syrup is chilling.

3
Strip the rest of the mint leaves from their stems. Toss the mint leaves with 1 teaspoon lemon juice and the oil.

4
Remove the syrup from the refrigerator and strain. Divide the strawberries between serving dishes and decorate with the mint leaves. Pour over the pepper syrup. Sprinkle with demerara or coarse sugar and serve (or serve the sugar separately).

CHEF'S ADVICE
Be sure to choose the finest strawberries in season. The sweetest strawberries tend to be available in June, which corresponds with the peppermint season quite nicely. This is a very summery recipe which can be prepared through the early days of Autumn.

Berry Sabayon
with Bourbon Vanilla

Preparation: 25 minutes
Cooking time: 15 minutes
Serves 4

FOR THE VANILLA SABAYON
1 small orange
4 egg yolks
50 g/1 3/4 oz caster sugar
100 ml/3 1/2 fl oz milk
4 pinches powdered Bourbon
vanilla
1 tablespoon kirsch

FOR THE BERRIES
200 g/7 oz strawberries
80 g/2 3/4 oz raspberries
80 g/2 3/4 oz redcurrants
80 g/2 3/4 oz blueberries
35 g/1 1/4 oz icing sugar

1
Gently rinse the berries and pat dry. Divide among 4 small gratin or ovenproof dishes.

2
Prepare the sabayon: Grate 1 tablespoon orange zest, then squeeze the juice. Prepare a large pot of boiling water for the water bath.

3
In a bowl, whisk together the egg yolks and sugar. Add the milk, vanilla, kirsch and orange zest. Set the bowl over the hot water which you should keep warm over low heat. Whisk the milk mixture until it becomes thick and frothy. Preheat the grill.

4
Pour the sabayon mixture over the fruit and sprinkle with icing sugar. Put the gratin dishes under the grill to caramelise lightly on top. Serve immediately.

Spice notes
Bourbon vanilla adds a peppery, tropical flower aroma that mingles to perfection with the velvety smoothness of the sabayon. Just a few pinches of Bourbon vanilla powder will transform an ordinary custard or creamy pudding. Try it also mixed into plain thick fromage frais for a simple and delicious dessert.

CHEF'S ADVICE
Serve this with thick slices of brioche bread that have been buttered, sprinkled with icing sugar and run under the grill to toast lightly. This sabayon is also good over sliced peeled citrus fruit, but replace the vanilla with cinnamon.

flowers, pods and seeds

tonka bean *Grate over desserts.*

cinnamon sticks *Use to flavour lamb, stewed fruit, jam and chutney.*

FLOWER PISTILS, ORCHID PODS, TREE BARK, strange beans, stems and seeds; spices come from some very unusual places.

In Kashmir, in Iran, in Spain and in central France, five hundred flowers from the *crocus sativus*, with 3 pistils each, must be gathered by hand to yield one gram of pure saffron. This precious gram comes in the form of a violet thread which turns yellow in contact with water and which adds amazing depth of flavour tinged with bitterness to fish soups, rice and scented oils. Vanilla pods, whose beautiful tiny black specks float deliciously atop many a dessert, is another spice treasure. They come from a tropical vine native to Central America and, along with chillies, were used to flavour Aztec hot chocolate. Transplanted to Reunion Island, the *vanilla fragrans* plants lacked the "melipones" bees of the Mexican jungle and would only flower if fertilised by hand. The green pods must first ferment, turn black and finally dry before becoming coated with tiny crystals of succulent vanillin. Vanilla from Tahiti is smooth and highly perfumed. Vanilla from Reunion Island,

vanilla pods

*Should be supple. The spice
of desserts, but also for
deliccte-fleshed fish and shellfish.*

lemongrass stalks

and dried lemongrass add exotic flavour to dishes.

powdered vanilla *The whole pod is dried and ground to a fine powder.*   **pain d'epices seasoning** *Cinnamon, ginger, anise.*

house blends

saffron *The finest threads have a deep crimson colour. Use for bouillabaisse, paella, red mullet and desserts.*

poppy seeds
Their nutty flavour goes well with salads, breads and tarts.

sesame seeds *Sweet in salads and crunchy when added to breaded coatings.*

also called Bourbon vanilla, is more peppery. When ground, it has a flavour that lingers on the palate.

Cinnamon comes from the bark of a tree in the laurel family. Thin layers of bark are scraped from the tree during the rainy season and left to dry, first in the shade, then in the sun. As they dry out, they roll up and fill the air with a delicious scent of honey and wood. Ground cinnamon is used for Moroccan pastries and, along with ginger and anise, to flavour biscuits and spice breads. True cinnamon originated in Sri Lanka but is also grown in India and Indonesia. It is not the same as cassia, which is remarkably similar but comes from China.

Tonka beans come from a tree native to Guyana. Originally used for medicinal purposes, and as a flavour enhancer, it is now recognised for its own aromas of cocoa, caramel and anise.

The long thin stem and small bulb of lemongrass is often chopped finely and sprinkled over Thai salads. Dried, ground lemongrass retains its lemony flavour with a hint of gingery bite.

Tiny sesame seeds, with a slightly nutty taste, add flavour and texture to pan-fried fish, bread and many pastries and desserts.

The blue-black seeds of a poppy flower can be sprinkled over salads and brioche.

Tonka Bean Truffles

**Preparation: 1 hour
(one day in advance)
Cooking time: 10 minutes
(in 2 sessions)
Makes about 50 truffles**

1/2 orange
1 tonka bean
150 ml/5 1/2 fl oz cream
370 g/13 oz best dark
chocolate (77%)
60 g/2 1/4 oz chestnut honey
20 g/3/4 oz unsalted butter
250 g unsweetened cocoa powder

Spice notes

**The pleasant caramelised, anise
flavour of the tonka mellows
the flavour of the dark chocolate,
balancing the taste quite nicely.
Do not be tempted to add too
much as this spice loses its
subtleness in large doses.**

I
One day before serving, grate the orange zest.
Grind the tonka bean in a spice mill. Coarsely chop
180 g/6 oz chocolate and put in a bowl.

2
Make a ganache by bringing the cream to the boil with
the orange zest and honey. Add 4 pinches of Tonka
powder (save the rest for another recipe). Slowly pour
the hot cream over the chopped chocolate. Set aside.

3
When the ganache is warm, add the butter cut in small
pieces. Set aside at room temperature for 12 hours.

4
The day of serving, form the ganache into balls using
a small spoon and your fingers to shape. Refrigerate
the balls for 1 hour.

5
Melt the remaining chocolate in a water bath and let
cool slightly.

6
Put the cocoa powder in a bowl. Dip the chocolate
balls first in the melted chocolate then roll in the
cocoa powder to coat.

CHEF'S ADVICE
*If you put the ganache balls in the freezer for 10 minutes before
dipping in chocolate they will have more of a crunch. It will be
easier to dip and coat the ganache balls if you are wearing gloves.
These truffles will keep for several days in an airtight container.
Serve with after-dinner coffee, or afternoon tea.*

Tuiles with Almond
and Szechuan Pepper

**Preparation: 30 minutes
(plus 1 hour resting time)
Cooking time: 10 minutes per batch
Makes about 18 tuile biscuits**

2 egg whites
1/2 lemon
25 g/1 oz unsalted butter
Whole Szechuan peppercorns
120 g/4 oz caster sugar
Bourbon vanilla powder
20 g/3/4 oz flour
120 g/4 oz slivered almonds

Spice notes
**The Szechuan pepper bursts
into a thousand resinous specks
which brings out the light buttery,
vanilla aroma of these biscuits.
Try a pinch of ground Szechuan
pepper to lift a madeira cake or
rice pudding out of the ordinary.**

1
Put the egg whites in a bowl and let stand at room
temperature while you prepare the other ingredients.
Grate the lemon zest. Melt the butter. Crush or
grind 1/4 teaspoon of the peppercorns.

2
Gently mix the egg whites with the sugar, lemon zest
and pinch of vanilla powder. Add the melted butter
and stir until thoroughly combined. Add the flour
and almonds. Let rest in the refrigerator for 1 hour.

3
Preheat the oven to 180° C/350° F. Spread spoonfuls
of the mixture very thinly in a circular shape on
a teflon baking sheet. Dip the back of the spoon
in water if necessary to prevent the dough from
sticking while you spread. Sprinkle each with a bit
of ground pepper.

4
Cook until just golden, about 10 minutes. Remove
immediately to cool and begin the next batch. Repeat
until all the batter is gone.

CHEF'S ADVICE
*Leave a gap between each dough circle, about 4 cm/1 in, to allow
for spreading. The size of the circles will depend on how big you
want your tuiles to be. For a traditional rounded shape, put the hot
tuiles straight from the oven onto a rolling pin to cool.*

Peach-Szechuan Pepper Jam

**Preparation: 25 minutes
(one day in advance)
Cooking time: 25 minutes
Keeping time: 3 months
Makes 4 250 g/9 oz jars**

550 g/1 1/4 lb yellow peaches
550 g/1 1/4 lb white peaches
1 lemon
850 g/2 lb preserving sugar
1/2 teaspoon Szechuan pepper

Spice notes
**The pairing of delicate peaches
and powerful pepper is not as
mismatched as it sounds. Quite
the opposite; the tender fruit
is crying out for the lemon
aroma of the Szechuan pepper,
which becomes almost floral
in contact with the honeyed
sweetness of the peaches.**

1
One day before, plunge the peaches into boiling water, then remove and plunge into cold water to cover and peel immediately. Remove the stones and cut into 5 mm/ 1/4 in slices.

2
Put the fruit in a preserving pan (or heavy casserole). Grate over the lemon zest and squeeze in the juice. Add the sugar. Cook until the mixture just bubbles, then add the pepper. Transfer to a bowl and refrigerate overnight.

3
Sterilise the jars and dry thoroughly.

4
With a slotted spoon, lift out the peach slices, leaving the juice in the pan. Cook the peach juice until it reaches 105° C/220° F on a sugar thermometer.

5
Return the peaches to the pan and bring to the boil (watch out for splatters). Skim off any foam that rises to the surface. Let simmer for 5-6 minutes. Transfer to the pots and seal.

CHEF'S ADVICE
If you do not have a sugar thermometer, drop a blob of the peach juice on a small plate. It should set within a few seconds; if not, continue cooking. Store this jam in a cool dark place for up to 3 months.

Dried Fruit Jam with Spices

Preparation: 25 minutes
Cooking time: 15-20 minutes
Keeping time: 3 months
Makes 3 250 g/9 oz jars

1 orange
2 lemons
75 g/2 3/4 oz almonds
75 g/2 3/4 oz walnuts
200 g/7 oz dried figs
100 g/3 1/2 oz dried apricots
50 g/1 3/4 oz dates
50 g/ 1 3/4 oz prunes
300 g/11 oz preserving sugar
1 cinnamon stick
4 cardamom pods
1 star anise
50 g/1 3/4 oz sultanas

Spice notes
The combination of cinnamon, cardamom and star anise is harmonious; it is at once floral, woody and herbal, with each aroma coming to the forefront in its turn. These spices lend a warm, enveloping, wintry note alongside the candied fruit taste, reminiscent of European gingerbread.

1
Sterilise the jars and dry thoroughly. Grate the zests of the orange and 1 lemon and squeeze the juices of both. Preheat the oven to 180° C/350° F.

2
Spread the almonds and walnuts on a baking sheet. Bake for 15 minutes to toast. Let cool. Cut the figs and apricots into quarters. Stone the dates and prunes and cut in half.

3
Bring 750 ml/1 25 fl oz water to the boil with the sugar, citrus zest and juice, and the spices. Add all the dried fruit. Simmer gently for 5 minutes, then raise the heat.

4
Boil briskly for 8 minutes. Add the walnuts and almonds and cook until it reaches 105° C/220° F on a sugar thermometer (or see Peach–Szechuan Pepper Jam, page 164). Transfer to the jars and seal. Store for up to 3 months in a cool dark place.

CHEF'S ADVICE
This jam has a delicious candied fruit taste and is ideal spread on thick slices of toasted buttered bread. It can also be served with baked pears or apples, or with crumbles.

Morello Cherry Chutney

**Preparation: 25 minutes
(2 days in advance)
Cooking time: 25 minutes
Makes 1 250 g/9 oz jar**

400 g/14 oz morello cherries
1 lime
60 g/2 1/4 oz caster sugar
4 tablespoons balsamic
vinegar
8 allspice berries
1 cinnamon stick
1 clove
2 pinches ground ginger

Spice notes

The tartness of the cherries and vinegar complement the woody, lemony tones of the allspice and clove. The addition of cinnamon makes this almost dessert-like (try it with vanilla or cinnamon ice cream, or with Gingerbread Spice Ice Cream, see page 136). The other spices tend toward the savoury, making this ideal with roast pork, poultry or game.

1
Stone the cherries and cut 1 slice from the lime.

2
In a heavy casserole, combine the cherries, spices, vinegar, lime slice and sugar. Bring to the boil, skim off any foam that rises, then lower the heat and simmer gently, covered, for 10 minutes.

3
Uncover and cook until the liquid is syrupy, about 10-15 minutes. Pour into a clean jar and cover. Refrigerate until needed.

CHEF'S ADVICE
Any type of cherry can be used for this recipe, and each variety will lend its own unique flavour. After opening, this will keep 2-3 weeks in the refrigerator. Store unopened jars in the refrigerator for up to 3 months.

overleaf
poppy seeds, lemon zest

Chocolate Sauce
with Tahitian Vanilla

Preparation: 10 minutes
Cooking time: 1 minute
Serves 4

40 g/ 1 1/2 oz best
dark chocolate
150 ml/5 1/2 fl oz cream
50 ml/ 1 3/4 fl oz milk
50 g/1 3/4 oz caster sugar
1/2 teaspoon Tahitian vanilla
10 g/1/2 oz unsalted butter

Spice notes
**With its creamy velvety taste,
Tahitian vanilla is the pure
essence of smoothness. Other
spices which blend well with
the fruity bitterness of chocolate
include ginger, star anise
and Pain d'épices seasoning.**

1
Finely chop the chocolate in a spice mill. In a pan,
combine the cream, milk and sugar and bring to
the boil. Remove from the heat and add the vanilla.

2
Pour the cream mixture into the chocolate in
three batches, stirring to blend. Let cool, then add
the butter, mixing with an immersion mixer.
Serve warm or cool.

CHEF'S ADVICE
*This sauce is perfect for any kind of chocolate cake, or with baked
apples or pears.*

Four Spice Blend Caramels

Preparation: 45 minutes
Cooking time: 10 minutes
Makes about 50 caramels

200 ml/7 fl oz cream
5 pinches fine Brittany sea salt
(fleur de sel)
1 tablespoon grated
orange zest
1/2 teaspoon Four Spice blend
20 g/3/4 oz acacia honey
280 g/ 10 oz caster sugar
40 ml/1 1/2 fl oz balsamic
vinegar
30 g/1 oz unsalted butter
Oil

Spice notes
**The flavours of the white pepper,
nutmeg, cinnamon and clove are
well-suited to the creamy texture
of the caramel. No one spice
dominates, and the combination
of milky, lightly orange-scented
caramel is reminiscent of
old-fashioned nursery puddings.**

1
Place a large sheet of baking parchment on a marble board or heatproof surface. Oil 3 metal square rulers and arrange on the paper about 1 inch apart.

2
Bring the cream to the boil. Remove from the heat and add the salt, orange zest and Four Spice blend.

3
In a heavy casserole, warm the honey and gradually add the sugar, stirring constantly with a wooden spoon. Cook until it turns a golden caramel colour. Remove from the heat and carefully stir in the vinegar and butter.

4
Gradually pour the warm cream into the caramel mixture, stirring. Bring to the boil over high heat, stirring constantly. To test for doneness, put the tip of a small knife into the caramel, dip the caramel into cold water and then taste. It should be soft but not too sticky.

5
Let cool slightly, then pour onto the parchment, using the rulers as guides. Let cool, then cut the caramel into bite-size squares.

CHEF'S ADVICE
Tilt the edges of the paper to prevent the caramel from oozing outside the rulers. These can be kept in airtight containers.

recipe index

spice index*

Numbers in bold indicate photographs

* Spices should be stored in a dark, dry place.

Acknowledgements

Marianne Paquin would like to thank for their assistance with photography :
Sandrine Ganem, Palais Royal and Quartz.

This edition published 2003 by
©Hachette Illustrated UK, Octopus Publishing Group
2-4 Heron Quays
London E14 4JP
CIP Data available
ISBN 1-84430-004-8

Editor: Colette Véron
Art director: Nancy Dorking
Layout: Séverine Morizet
English adaptation: Rachida Zerroudi
Translator: Laura Washburn

Photogravure: EURESYS à Baisieux